Lord, You Know I Can't Hear!

Practical Solutions for People with Hearing Loss

David M. Harrison

Disclaimer: I am not a doctor, audiologist or a scientist, but I am a person with hearing loss desperately seeking solutions and answers to improve hearing. Some ideas were developed in the Lip Reading Academy while teaching others methods of communication.

I am a crusader campaigning for hearing accessibility. I move with an evangelistic fervor proclaiming the need to help those with hearing loss.

The author and publisher have made every effort to ensure that the information in this book was correct at press time. The author and publisher do not assume and hereby disclaim any liability to any party for any loss, damage or disruption caused by errors or omissions, whether such error or omissions result from negligence, accident or any other cause.

All scripture quotations are taken from the King James Version

Printed in the United States of America

ISBN 978-1-941749-35-7

4-P Publishing

Chattanooga, Tennessee

Cover artwork Copyright ©2015 David M. Harrison

Cover design and photography by Kat Morris

Editing by Sylvia S. Banks

Proofreading by Cathy Hart Harrison

"It is the supreme art of the teacher to awaken joy in creative expression and knowledge." Einstein

"The man who can make a hard thing easy is the educator."

Connect with David

E-mail: letmypeoplehear@yahoo.com

Visit my Website: www.letmypeoplehear.com

Phone: 423-624-1669

Mailing Address: P.O. Box 3021 ~ Chattanooga, TN 37404

Order your Magic Hearing Buttons today. Sold in pairs in case you lose one. Full instructions are included with every set. Pin it on and let it begin working for you.

Cost $5.00+ $2.00 for shipping. Total $7.00
Send money order to **Let My People Hear, Inc**. with your name & address to P.O. Box 3021 Chattanooga, TN 37404

Order online: letmypeoplehear.com then click Button

Contact letmypeoplehear@yahoo.com or 423-624-1669

Foreword

I t has been in recent years that I have been closely acquainted with those who have a hearing loss. These individuals have not allowed their disability to dictate their destiny. I am inspired and amazed at their strength to overcome obstacles and pursue their purpose and make incredible impacts. To me, these individuals are not handicapped but "handi-capable."

I believe David Harrison has authored a book that sheds light on a topic that is not often discussed. However, the statistics of those with hearing loss are quite alarming and leads me to conclude that too many are suffering because of their silence.

Through this book, a voice has been given for the hearing impaired and challenges all of us to step up to the plate. We need to become sensitive to the needs of those with hearing loss and be advocates for them. It is a mission field, and it could very well be our neighbor or someone in our community who needs to know someone cares.

It teaches friends with hearing loss how they can hear. Applying these techniques and strategies will enhance your quality of life and create opportunities. It also teaches those of us who don't have a hearing loss better ways for us to communicate with our friends and include them in our conversations, classes, church services and conferences.

As you read the book, you will be inspired and challenged. Get ready for a hearing tune up!

Sylvia Banks

Family Manager Coach

What you will discover in this book is that 20% of churchgoers have hearing loss. This means that a significant amount of communication is lost, causing those with hearing loss to feel excluded by those who don't suffer hearing loss.

Friends with hearing loss can use auditory training to make the most of residual hearing, using visual training to let their eyes supplement what they hear. They can develop a simple method of teaching themselves lip reading or speech reading.

Those with and those without hearing loss can become proactive about the need to hear and to understand what people are saying; people without hearing loss can be understanding, and assist those with hearing loss. Do not take hearing for granted, thinking one can get by without help from others; one can't hide hearing loss with the most expensive hearing aids or best cochlear implants in the world. This book will help you develop a whole new dimension of better communication.

Eric Peterson, writer

Contents

Acknowledgments/Dedication

I owe it all to my wonderful Lord and Savior Jesus Christ, who revealed this ministry to me in January 2006.

To my dear wife, Cathy of 51 years who pursued with great patience with a husband with a hearing loss.

To Rev. Loren Bjokne of Cottage Grove Baptist Church, Cottage Grove, Minnesota, for seeing the vision and inspiring me to develop this ministry in 2006.

To Rev. Humphreys of Edgewood Baptist Church, who made the church hearing accessible for me to attend.

To the Honorable Former Mayor Pat Rose, Chattanooga, TN, for opening a pilot program Bible class for hearing accessibility.

To Dr. David Myers, Missionary Director of Hamilton County, who organized a pastor's conference on hearing accessibility in the church.

To Dr. Ted Camp, Director of Silent Word Ministries, Inc. who helped me to find my niche in ministry.

To Fred Brewer at Westside Baptist Church, who prayed the prayer that became the heart cry for this book.

To Pastor Tony Walliser of Silverdale Baptist Church for encouraging us to establish a Hearing Center to reach out to the hearing impaired

To all our dear friends who pray for the hearing loss population around the world as a mission field.

About the Author

D avid M Harrison was born hard of hearing and struggled to hear and communicate all his life. In 1995, he dropped out of church because it was not hearing accessible.

In January 2006, Harrison spent fourteen days in fasting and prayer seeking desperately to resolve his hearing dilemma.

In his research, he came across the statistics that there were 36 million Americans with hearing loss but only 500,000 were deaf and spoke sign language. Today there are 50 million Americans with mild to profound hearing loss in need of help to deal with it. That is one out of every five.

At that time, a website popped up that changed the course of his life. It was the site of "The American Academy for Hearing Loss Support Specialists." It was an online academic study on helping others cope with hearing loss.

David and his wife Cathy, a registered nurse, took the studies and learned to train hard of hearing people in social, conversational and communication skills.

They have become crusaders and advocates for hearing accessibility in the workplace, schools, hospitals, public venues and church.

In 2013 Let My People Hear became certified as a 501 (c) (3) non-profit organization. We are now able to raise support and funds for special mission projects for children, teens and adults.

The dream began in January 2006 and grew. He says, "A dream is an opportunity to do the impossible. Persistence makes the impossible possible. Once a dream has been planted in your heart it has no expiration date."

Preface

The title of this book is that of a desperate prayer from a deacon with hearing loss. It could well be your plea and the prayer of millions of friends like you who suffer a hearing disability. In 2006, I cried out in agony to God in prayer, regarding my diminishing hearing. My passion for finding a solution led me to spend fourteen days in prayer and fasting, the best thing I did for the cause of hearing loss. Many miracles have since unfolded.

My first answer to prayer came from the American Academy of Hearing Loss Support Specialists. My wife, Cathy, a nurse, and I enrolled in the studies on January 20, 2006 and discovered a whole new world of communication. We completed the academic training to become hearing loss support specialists.

In 2007, we founded the Lip Reading Academy and taught scores of people about their hearing needs, and ways they could benefit from this instruction. This book unveils several amazing strategies and methods that can improve your communication skills, even as much as 30%. With practice, you can apply these methods.

I feel overwhelmed at the birth of this book. It is a miracle, my life's dream, love, and passion. I share it with you who have hearing loss, people I care about, who need help with understanding hearing loss.

David M. Harrison

1

The Quest for a Hearing Loss Solution

My Parent's Quest

When a child is born with a handicap, the parents begin a quest for answers and solutions. The quest for a cure becomes a never-ending process to fix.

A first-born son, with a hearing twin brother, I was born with a profound hearing loss. Before I could speak and hear how to pronounce words, I was mislabeled by schools as retarded. The belief at that time was deaf and hard of hearing children were unteachable and mentally incompetent. I attended special education classes until the ninth grade, then mainstreamed, which was hard. It was difficult for my parents dealing a child with hearing loss; they blamed each other for my loss of hearing. Each one searched for a cure or solution to restore my hearing. Mom conferred with the medical profession while Dad sought a cure with alternative methods.

> **The belief at that time was deaf and hard of hearing children were unteachable and mentally incompetent.**

Mother's Quest

When I was four, Mom was told to have my tonsils removed because they could affect hearing in children. Our family moved from rural Southern Minnesota to the big city to find the best medical help. I endured many trips to ear specialists who performed painful exams and experiments. One experiment was swallowing water while the doctor blew air into my nose to clear out the passageway. Another procedure was to spray Novocain into my nostrils.

I spent a day at the University of Minnesota Medical School for experiments. A verbal hearing test took place, consisting of 100 words. A person stood behind me saying these words, and I was to select the correct word. The test was repeated with me wearing a set of headphones. The person spoke these words into a microphone, which was out of my sight. On both of these tests, my score was 90% wrong. If the person had faced me and said these words, the score would have been 90% right.

One frightening experiment was entering a soundproof room that looked like a vault, with a very thick door and very small window. Inside were strange looking cones on the wall and ceiling. The experiment was perhaps various sounds at a range of tones and volumes. Outside the door, there were people with white lab coats writing reports and looking at machines.

Next, I was ushered into a large room with a conference table and glass windows from floor to ceiling, looking out onto University Avenue in Minneapolis. On the other side of the room stood a wall of mirrors from floor to ceiling. Several children sat around the table with microphones. The leader sat at one end of the table and interacted with the children. I sat at the far end. I cannot remember what we discussed that day, but when I spoke up to answer a question, my answer was followed by a roar of laughter. I felt very confused about what had happened. When the session was over, I discovered that behind the wall of mirrors was an amphitheater filled with spectators.

Dad's Quest

Dad had an alternative view of curing hearing loss. One of them was an electrostatic device, used for various types of healing including hearing loss. John Wesley, the founder of the Methodist Church denomination, was the first to use it. Few know he was one of the first persons in England to use a static electricity machine to heal many disorders, including blindness, gout, sprains, deafness, toothaches, and stomach and back pain. Wesley wrote in his book, Primitive Physick (written in 1747; his name was added as author in 1760), that electricity is "the nearest to universal medicine, of any yet known in the world." Primitive Physick was an inexpensive guide to simple, safe, effective cures, containing 900 recipes and cures for

288 afflictions. The book was so popular and published in 32 updated editions.

My dad and my Aunt Rose had their ideas of what would give me hearing. Grandpa Martin B. Harrison owned the farm that had the famous Indian "Jeffers Petroglyphs," the oldest and largest surviving concentration of Native American rock art in the Upper Midwest. The farm had a natural spring of pure water, and Indian tribes came to visit the petroglyph. Aunt Rose learned about the medicine and cures for various ailments. I was given something to drink and a ritual from the medicine man to restore my hearing. Aunt Rose knew traveling evangelists who practiced faith healing, and they prayed over me. Years later, when we visited a Pentecostal church, the pastor saw my hearing aid. He insisted I could get rid of it and prayed for healing. I mostly recall his strong garlic breath.

The quest for healing went on, and Dad took me to a Palmer Chiropractor, who claimed she could heal my hearing loss. Chiropractic therapy originated in 1895 when D.D. Palmer claimed to have restored deaf janitor, Harvey Lillard's hearing by manipulating his spine. It makes no anatomical sense, and few if any chiropractors claim to reverse deafness today.

> It is not easy to accept any handicap.
> Hearing loss will not go away or be restored. The best solution is to find alternative methods of communication. We have to deal with it sooner or later.

Dr. Moe would stick her thumb in my ear canal and pull my ears several times. Harvey Lillard was the first and only man cured of hearing loss by Palmer, and no one has ever heard of another hearing loss healing. There were plenty of herbal practitioners around to offer their suggestions and sell their products, but all to no avail for a cure for me.

My sister Marlene, remembers the Rife Machine treatment of which I have no recollection. In 1932, Dr. Royal Rife invented the Rife

Machine, which used frequencies, generated by his machine, to cure diseases. Dr. Rife found that every disease organism has a frequency range in which it can be affected, and that this is what he called its window of vulnerability. Dad heard about the famous 1934 clinic where 16 patients, recovered from cancer and some from tuberculosis by the use of these primary frequencies. Dad felt this machine would cure my hearing loss. I remember holding copper rods in my hands as frequencies went through my body, something to do with positive protons and negative electrons.

There was another treatment called electrostatic therapy. The hand-held unit emitted blue electrical sparks in a glass tube that passed over my head and body. The unit produced a strong ozone smell that comes after lightning and thunderstorm.

While I was in the fifth and sixth grade, speech therapists would take me out of the classroom once a week to teach me how to speak and pronounce words. There were lots of charts on word formations. I will always be grateful for that training.

It is not easy to accept any handicap. Hearing loss will not go away or be restored. The best solution is to find alternative methods of communication. We have to deal with it sooner or later.

My Personal Quest

I looked forward to our church service that morning as the church filled with excited worshipers. The singing was lively, prayers were heartfelt and the preaching powerful. A haunting thought entered my mind.

Being born with bilateral hearing loss, I never paid much attention to the words. It seemed a good thing to attend church and go through the motions and activities. "That was the normal thing to do," I thought. But something was missing, and it dawned on me in 1995 while attending church. The haunting question was, "What do I understand?"

Picking up a bulletin, I made notes on what I heard and understood that day. It proved a very shocking and devastating hour for me. Singing the hymns from the book was okay, as long as someone helped me find the page number since I could not hear the page number announced. Following the message while looking up scripture texts, or taking notes while lip reading was impossible for me.

During the prayer time, everyone reverently bowed their heads and closed their eyes. For me to peek and read lips would have been considered disrespectful. The person praying would bow his head making it hard for me to pray in spirit with him. The biggest shock came to me during the special music when I could not distinguish any words sung by the choir, groups, or individuals. Every song had a message that I could not comprehend.

> I felt like I had been delivered a "death" sentence on my life. Sometimes I referred to this as a "deaf" sentence, a separation from a hearing world of communication for the rest of my life.

My spirit was sinking fast as I asked myself, "What was I getting out of the worship service?" Apparently, I was not getting anything meaningful from the service.

After the service, I approached an associate pastor and shared the struggle to understand the message. His only reply was, "Do the best you can; we can't help you."

I felt like I had been delivered a "death" sentence on my life. Sometimes I referred to this as a "deaf" sentence, a separation from a hearing world of communication for the rest of my life. I left the church with a broken heart realizing that there were no solutions available at the time.

My family and others did not understand what was wrong with me as I became difficult to live with and bitter. I spent five years avoiding church and feeling depressed while developing a one-on-one ministry that I could handle well.

My wonderful, caring wife, Cathy, gave me an article from a magazine. It told how a movie star with hearing loss was encouraged by joining a support group called, Self Help for Hard of Hearing (SHHH), now known as Hearing Loss Associations of America. We joined the local monthly chapter and met many wonderful friends with hearing loss. Peer mentoring with others who understand hearing loss has been a great encouragement for each of us.

2

Mr. Brewer's Cry & Quest for Hearing

The monthly potluck dinner at the Westside Baptist Church drew Deacon Brewer to the night of fellowship, although he dreaded it. Hearing loss was quite an issue for him, and knowing the dinner would be in the church hall-a gymnasium filled with noise from people, machines, and echoing left him feeling a little despondent. He left his hearing aids at home, knowing of their uselessness in this setting. Not being able to hear, and not being able to engage fully among those at the meeting, bothered Mr. Brewer.

Once he was there, he enjoyed the meal; the food lovingly prepared, and the variety was pleasant. Observing the people dining, laughing and talking helped the meal go down, as well.

Then, the meeting started. The noise of the air conditioner, sound waves bouncing off the floor, the ceiling and back and then off the walls; and the

> He wasn't sorry he'd left his hearing aids at home. They would not have aided in his hearing loss tonight. But, oh, how he wished he could hear.

noise of people created a sound barrier for Mr. Brewer. He smiled, but he did not understand what was being said.

The meeting had three parts, the beginning, middle and end. At the close of the meeting, the chairperson arose and said, "We must pray for many things. Let's have three people to conclude our meeting in prayer."

The first prayer came from a man 20 feet away from Mr. Brewer. He keenly watched the man's lips moving but heard nothing.

The second prayer came from a man seated 18 feet away. It was the same as the first prayer, a voice too distant, noise all around, but utter silence to Mr. Brewer. He wasn't sorry he'd left his hearing aids at home. They would not have aided in his hearing loss tonight. But, oh, how he wished he could hear.

For the third prayer, the chairperson, called Mr. Brewer to conclude the evening. "Oh my," he thought, "what do I do, what can I say?" Nothing had been audible to him. Then came the embarrassment of being chosen, and having to demonstrate that he could not hear, or be a participant in the meeting because of a failure on his part, his hearing loss. Overcome by his thoughts and feelings, he became emotional and decided to be truthful.

"O Lord, you know I can't hear, I don't know what was said tonight. I'm hard of hearing. I don't know what or for whom I'm supposed to pray. Whatever requests were given, bless every one of them." Being truthful, he felt emboldened and prayed again, "Lord, hear my cry; I can't hear!" I want to hear everything but can't understand the words, and missed all the prayer requests. You know what they are; please bless every one of them. Amen."

Before we look at the story, let's look at impairments, for those with hearing and those who have hearing loss. Every person in life will have blind spots and should be seeking and learning what and where each blind spot may be. If the blind spot is hindering a more spiritual and emotional wellness, this can be referred to as spiritual and emotional defecit.

In a way, an image or question might be, what "pushups" do I have to do to make my life more spiritually and emotionally fit? Those with hearing loss have an added challenge before them, to find and maintain this fitness. They have to communicate their needs and find "community" within the church. They must find community among those who do not have hearing loss, those who do have hearing loss and recognize the issue and even those who have hearing loss and choose not to recognize the issue.

This chapter, specifically, addresses issues for those who have hearing loss. These issues are also common in those without hearing loss, because it's part of what it means to be human, pursuing an emotional and spiritually fit life. Desiring the serenity and peace, which comes from seeking and finding God's will for us. In other words, His plan and sense of direction should be our mission.

The first step for those with hearing loss is to "admit the issue," and to take into account that this may be hindering you from a better quality of life. To understand the extent of your hearing loss, one must see an audiologist and take an audiogram test. This test measures the ability to hear volume (loudness), and sensitivity, the high and low frequencies in both ears.

Once the hearing loss is acknowledged, then ignorance is no longer an issue. The next step is to take personally the initiative and learn how to ask for help from others. It is not as easy as it seems. Mr. Brewer's story illustrates some of these areas that we will examine in this chapter. It is considered denial when one chooses not to understand the importance of hearing loss or refuses to ask for help.

> **Those who choose to ignore their hearing loss begin to place barriers, hindering the possibility of having a better and more spiritually fit life.**

Let's examine the barriers placed. Mr. Brewer attended the church fellowship with others, knowing he had trouble with his hearing. He went thinking he could pretend to hear, knowing a despondency affected his spirit, but he went regardless. He felt, regardless of what little he could hear, there would at least be value in being with his friends, those who were not aware of his hearing loss. He would pretend to hear. That would be sufficient enough.

The next part of Mr. Brewer's story is being called upon to pray. He was expected to follow suit of those who had prayed ahead of him. However, not having heard their prayers, he was caught "on the spot". He had no idea what the prayer requests had been nor did he know how to add to the previous prayers. This situation would be rather embarrassing for anyone.

This embarrassing moment led Mr. Brewer to the feeling of frustration, a natural emotion. He had to admit that he had not heard the conversations at the meeting and was only pretending to hear. It is possible that frustration could have pushed the button for the next emotion of anger to arise. Possibly posing the question, "Why God, me? Why do I have this hearing loss?" It is the natural progression of thought and emotion for those with hearing loss, as is evident in Mr. Brewer's story. If he had acquired the skill to lip read and had shared his hearing loss with his friends, that night might have ended differently. Those who were speaking or praying could have easily solved the problem by simply facing Mr. Brewer so he could read their lips and take part in the meeting by "hearing" what was being said.

Unfortunately, too often, fear and ignorance are barriers that can leave one helpless and hopeless. Asking for help is making an admission: that I don't have the same hearing as others, this can be embarrassing for some. The fear of rejection, afraid that I might face rejection when asking for help or even possibly, refused help. Ignorance of the issue, hearing loss, keeps one from discovering solutions, such as lip reading. Because of fear and ignorance Mr. Brewer's spiritual and emotional fitness, his communion with God and self-esteem were all affected; his serenity was no more.

Fear must be addressed and overcome. Otherwise, it will lead to unhealthy thoughts, such as: "What's the use; no one will understand," or "I'll deal with the issue tomorrow." Burying your head in the sand or procrastinating will not improve your situation. It will only affect your spiritual and emotional well-being.

Address fear so isolation does not also compound the situation. Loneliness and solitude should not be confused: the first leads to loss of self-esteem, and the second is a part of a healthy spiritual life. When the here and now cease to matter, one can choose solitude to commune individually with God.

All of these emotions will lead to despair and despondency, a sense of sadness and joylessness and eventually into depression. Depression is usually preceded by anxiety. Anxiety is the feeling of uneasiness of mind asking questions such as: "What can I do? Is there anything that can be done? What if nothing can be done?" These anxious questions can drive one into utter depression as if straying from the "right road," and finding one's self in darkness and desperately seeking the light. Where is the answer?

This depression is not yours alone. It affects others too, most often those who are near to you and usually that is your family. They don't suffer hearing loss; only you do, so how could they possibly understand what you are experiencing? How do you explain the significance of something to someone who can never possibly know what is important to you? And worse yet, would the family member, if he/she did have hearing loss, would it be the same significance to him/her as it is to you? This paralyzing train of thought can go in so many directions at once and can seemingly never end. Also, your friends who don't have hearing loss, will not understand the depression or reason for it. They may tell you to "snap out of it". They may try to shout to make you hear them, not realizing this is not the solution.

I am reminded of a friend, who tells the story of being in Germany with his relatives. He's an American, and while he was with his German relative he happened to witness another American trying to communicate with a German citizen. The American did not speak German, and the German did not speak English. The American asked the German a question, the German did not understand the question because he did not understand English.

What do you think happened next? The American realized the German didn't understand his question. So, the American raised his voice, speaking louder, almost too loud and still in English, thinking that this would make the German understand his question. Well, you can guess the outcome. The German still did not understand and was left with an impression of an ugly, loud American tourist.

3

What is Hearing Loss?

The human ear is capable of recognizing nearly 500,000 distinct sounds. However, not everyone can hear all of these sounds. A hearing loss exists when a person has a diminished sensitivity to the sounds normally heard. The term hearing impairment describes people who have relative insensitivity to sound in different speech frequencies. The severity of hearing loss is categorized according to the increase in volume that must be made above the usual level before the listener can detect it. It is also known as a hearing threshold, indicated by the range of the quietest sound that a person can detect. This threshold can accurately be measured by an audiogram. Another aspect to hearing loss involves the perceived clarity of a sound rather than its volume. Hearing tests have been designed to measure one's ability to understand speech, in volume and clarity of sound.

So that I can show how this applies to hearing loss, I have designed a simple layman's version of measurements of audio levels from an audiogram. I drew this picture of the ear, the cochlear unfolded, to help you understand how and where the hearing loss occurs. The ear is designed to hear different sounds at different points or stages in the cochlear. Hearing loss takes place when damage to the cochlear happens. The cochlear contains about 15 to 20 thousand tiny hair cells. These hair cells receive sounds at different frequencies. The cochlear sends the received sound to the brain by electric impulse, which the brain interprets.

The Hearing Chart

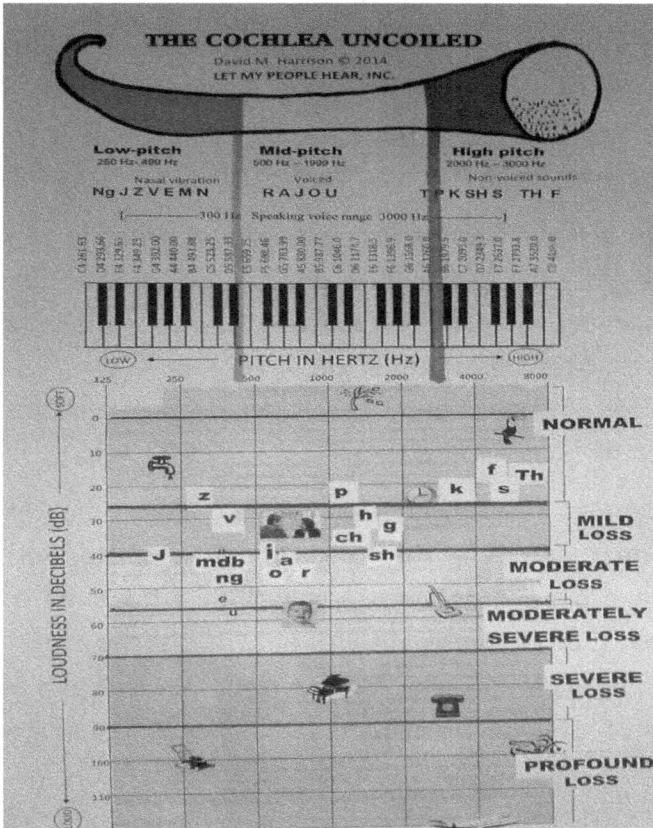

Hearing loss is divided into five levels according to the chart. For the decibel levels mentioned, refer to this chart.

The first level of hearing loss is *Mild Hearing Loss*. The most sensitive hair cells and high-frequency cells are near the entrance to the oval window. Trauma, high fever, some medications, and loud noises or music can cause damage to these cells.

If you have a mild hearing loss, it can cause some difficulty following speech sounds in a noisy environment. The quietest sounds you can detect are between 25 to 39 decibels (dB). It means that you are already missing some of the non-voiced sounds or the high pitched consonants such as t, p, k, sh, th, and f. These sounds are critical in understanding words.

It is the level that I call selective hearing. You make mistakes and slide over it. Other people know you are misunderstanding words but pass it off as a joke. However, all hearing loss is serious and needs to be addressed.

The second level of hearing loss is *Moderate Hearing Loss*. People with moderate hearing loss have difficulty following a conversation of three or more people. The quietest sounds you can hear are in the range of 40 to 59 decibels (dB). You are missing some of the mid-pitch voiced vowel sounds. This person can miss up to 50-75% of a spoken message or discussion.

The third level of hearing loss is *Moderately Severe Hearing Loss*. We can now hear sounds in the range of 55 to 69 decibels (dB) but cannot make out words. Not being able to hear the consonants makes most speech unintelligible. You will miss most of the spoken conversation, even if talking face to face. We depend on hearing aids, assistive listening devices and captioning as well as lip reading.

The fourth level of hearing loss is *Severe Hearing Loss*. We can hear sounds at levels between 70 to 89 decibels (dB). We may not even hear voices unless the speech is loud. Without amplification, an individual probably will not recognize any speech in a normal situation. With amplification, he/she may recognize some speech and detect some environmental sounds.

The fifth level of hearing loss is *Profound Hearing Loss*. You may not be able to hear sounds, but can feel some vibrations. You depend on vision as the primary means of communication which may include sign language.

 When you finally realize that you have a hearing loss, it is time to seek help and start learning to communicate in a way that produces understanding. Understand your communication needs and be able to explain how others can better communicate with you. Hearing loss in most cases is gradual and permanent. Once the damage is done, there is no way to reverse the process back to normal hearing. There are many things you can do to help yourself and your family to deal with the disability. Find a support group or start one. Get books on living with hearing loss. Become an advocate for hearing accessibility.

The Hearing Bubble

People with hearing loss live in a hearing bubble of communication. It is not a scientific study, rather some helpful ideas on how to deal with hearing loss. It was discovered by personal experience on what I hear clearly. It may help you understand your communication bubble.

My personal hearing range limits to a small area of three to five feet. Each person with hearing loss should determine his/her range of hearing. It is important that you are aware of your bubble of hearing all the time.

E no hearing zone

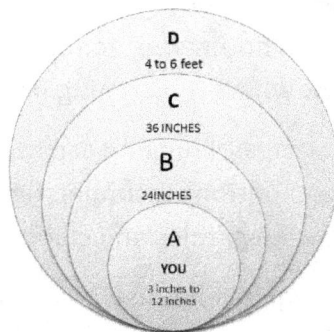

D
4 to 6 feet

C
36 INCHES

B
24INCHES

A
YOU
3 inches to
12 inches

F no hearing zone

"A" hearing zone. It is my personal hearing bubble without an amplifier. I can hear or comprehend most words up to twelve inches only if you are facing me and speaking normally.

"B" & "C" hearing zone. I can understand speech up to 36 inches with my amplifier when the speaker is facing me.

"D" is a difficult hearing zone for me to comprehend much even with my amplifier. What is shocking is that all hearing aids begin to fail in the four to six feet range. Those tiny little microphones the size of the tip of a ballpoint pen are not designed to pick up any clear speech signals beyond this area. Can those expensive units the size of a peanut deliver sound clearly for a person with severe to profound hearing loss?

Can those microphones pick up a whisper fifty feet away? Can they plow through all the noise pollution and pick out voices clearly? No matter how much you pay for those hearing aids you need to know the range that your unit can pick up pure tones. Do not depend only on the hearing unit to pick up all speech communication. This is why I advocate developing an alternative method of communication to augment your hearing unit.

"E & F" are no hearing zones. Any conversation beyond six feet and anything behind me are a no hearing zone. Sometimes I can hear a voice, but may not know where it is coming from or who is speaking.

Knowing your personal range of hearing can make a difference in confusion versus comprehension, misunderstanding versus understanding and between garbles and clarity in communication.

Listening to any range requires intense focus. It leads to exhaustion and mental fatigue. You can save a lot of time and energy by developing your limitations and boundaries hearing bubble. Share it with your family and friends.

Your inner circle of family and friends can be taught your hearing range when they speak to you. No two people have the same kind of hearing loss or special needs that come with their hearing bubble. Help your hearing friends adjust to your hearing needs accordingly.

Most friends with hearing loss must see the face of the one who is speaking. It is the only way to enhance their ability to understand what others are saying by 30%. There are communication helpers that are visible. What we miss with our ears, we may pick up with our eyes. Some of these communication aids are:

- Seeing the speaker face to face
- Observing facial expressions
- Watching the eyes
- Body language and gestures
- Lip reading
- Written text or captioning

An ENT (Ear, Nose, and Throat) doctor looking into my ear and asking me questions is a joke to me. I am there because I have a hearing problem, but he keeps on talking.

You are in the center of the hearing bubble. All communication revolves around you. I have discovered that a close range of three to six inches from my left ear, I can hear a normal voice and understand most of the conversation without lip reading. When someone begins to whisper without voicing, I cannot understand anything. There is a close range group of people that are impossible for me to understand. A dentist, a hygienist or medical doctors wearing a mask are difficult to understand. An ENT (Ear, Nose, and Throat) doctor looking into my ear and asking me questions is a joke to me. I am there because I have a hearing problem, but he keeps on talking. The eye doctor looks into my eyes at close range and reports to the Nurse four or five feet away to write numbers on my chart, but I cannot hear what he is saying. The barber or hair stylist tries to carry on a conversation with me, but my hearing aids are on the counter. The chiropractor or massage therapist talks to me, but they are always behind me. I can hear their voices, but I cannot understand their words clearly.

The Number 1 is my Good Hearing Zone. It is my normal conversational range where lip reading is part of it. It is where the magic hearing button method works best. We will cover this in another chapter. My best hearing range is arm's length from the side to the front. Yelling is not necessary, so please speak in a natural tone of voice. Yelling distorts words and is difficult to lip read. When understanding becomes difficult, I plug in my Williams Pocket Amplifier and extend my unit out to the speaker to pick out the voice.

Don't be afraid to ask people to move closer to speak into your microphone. Facts about the microphone are some of the hardest concepts to grasp. Place any microphone used in public within three to ten inches of the speaker's mouth. If the speaker moves more than a foot away from the microphone, guess what? There will be difficulty hearing.

TV personalities use lavaliere microphones clipped to the lapel or collars. These microphones are very expensive and yet they will not pick up sound more than a foot away.

In hearing aids manufactured today, the average microphone is smaller than the tip of a ballpoint pen. Can it be as powerful as the stage microphone in an auditorium? If you pay more money for a smaller hearing aid, will it help you hear more? Can an expensive hearing aid the size of a peanut deliver sound clearly for a person with a moderate to severe hearing loss?

Will the microphone pick up a whisper fifty feet away? Can these tiny microphones plow through all the noise pollution and pick out voices clearly? Above all this, we are surrounded by noise from every direction. We have to deal with echoes, reverberations, background noise, music, TVs and machinery everywhere.

If the lighting is poor or there are bright lights behind the speaker, this creates shadows on their faces. All these things are changing constantly and are very hard to control. In the classroom setting there comes a babble that makes it difficult to hear, learn and remember.

Several different microphones have multiple uses. The Williams Pocket Amplifier has a detachable microphone along with an extension cord for TV viewing. A conference microphone can be placed in the middle of a table enabling the one with the hearing loss to hear everyone seated around. A shotgun microphone is designed to pick up voices, fifteen to twenty feet away. It works well in a busy convention area. You can point the microphone at the speaker.

The number 2 area is my fair hearing zone. With my hearing aids, my range of communication is between three to five feet when the person talking is facing me. Most people do not understand what I can or cannot hear in a group situation like a classroom or family gathering.

The number 3 area is a poor no hearing zone. Beyond the five feet range, all conversation becomes garbled and undistinguishable.

The number 4 area is my very bad no hearing zone. It is when all speech is taking place behind me, or the speaker is out of sight. In this zone, nothing can be understood or comprehended. It is very difficult for most people to believe.

The number 5 area is my complete no hearing zone. Anyone speaking from another room or over an intercom system is out of my ear range. Only in my imagination can I guess at what is being said and who is talking.

The number 6 area is drawing your hearing zone. Determine your hearing zones and draw your circles of what you can hear in each zone. It is not a perfect way to determine your zones, but it can give you an idea where you are on the social network. It is important that you share your limitations.

Dad's story: Get in my Bubble

Dad's caregivers yelled at him continually because they thought he was not listening to them. Dad was almost 90 years old and was taken into our sister's home in Minnesota after Mother passed away.

Family, friends and caregivers assumed that yelling at Dad was the only way to communicate with him. Questions and instructions were repeated several times with increasing volume. The patience of the caregivers wore thin, and they thought Dad was giving them a hard time.

The yelling continued, and Dad would respond saying, "Stop yelling at me! I'm not deaf. I don't understand what you are saying." Dad often secluded himself in his room just to stay out of trouble and in fear of being placed in a nursing home.

In desperation, my sister phoned me in Chattanooga, Tennessee to come help care for Dad. I flew to Minnesota for a stay of several weeks. When I arrived, my sister came running out the door clutching her throat and greeted me with, "I have worn out my voice yelling at Dad for three days. I'm exhausted from trying to communicate with him!"

During the first few minutes I was there, I saw the problem and knew how to correct it. The caregivers were speaking outside of Dad's hearing range. Waving my hand for silence, I said, "Watch me." Walking over to Dad, I got his attention and looked directly into his face. In a natural tone of voice, I said, "Hi Dad, how are you?" He replied, "Fine." I proceeded with a few more questions to determine whether he understood me clearly. I asked one more question, "Why is she yelling at you?" His answer was, "I don't know why, but it sure hurts like heck when she does."

What was the problem? No one took the time to slow down and come around in front of Dad to speak face to face with him. He would have been able to hear and also to read their lips.

Every caregiver in nursing homes, hospitals, and senior facilities could and should learn from this. We need to change the way we communicate with those who have hearing loss. This principle can be applied in the home, school, church and workplace. A little effort goes a long way in communicating with people with hearing loss.

Getting into the hearing bubble reduces confusion and helps with cooperation. Talking from the side or behind a patient means miscommunication. Talking from more than six feet away can garble your message. Every person with hearing loss has a hearing range or bubble of hearing for better communication. Every time you speak, remember to enter into their bubble or hearing range.

Blind Spots of Hearing

4

Did you know there are "blind spots" to hearing where friends with hearing loss cannot understand what you are saying?

Truck drivers have at least four blind spots where most accidents happen. The driver's visibility at all times is of utmost importance for safety. The major responsibility for safety lies with those driving near the big trucks. We must be conscious of those blind spots around the truck and drive defensively.

On the back of a tractor trailer, I saw a small sign that read, "If you cannot see my mirrors, I cannot see you." From that sign, I coined the words, "If I cannot see your face, I cannot understand you." Hearing people need to understand where the blind spots or "no hear" areas of friends with hearing loss are and speak from the hearing areas.

It is not always the fault of the person with hearing loss that he cannot understand you as you speak. The major responsibility of good communication lies with the hearing person. Do not assume that if you are speaking from any point that you are fully understood.

The hard of hearing person's visibility of the speaker's face is of utmost importance at all times for better communication. Most arguments and anger escalates from no-hearing zones of the hard of hearing person. Be patient with us when we do not understand you. Move yourself into a better position for clarity.

People with hearing loss like me, live in a hearing bubble of communication. My personal hearing bubble range is a small area of three to five feet. Each person must determine his/her range of hearing. It is important that you are aware of your bubble area of hearing.

Your inner circle of family and friends can be taught your hearing range and improve communication with you. No two people have the same kind of hearing loss or special needs that come with their hearing bubble. Help your hearing friends adjust to your hearing needs.

Most friends with hearing loss must see the face of the one who is speaking. It is the only way to enhance their ability to understand what others are saying. It is almost like a magic hearing button, helping people to move away from your blind hearing spots and come face to face with you.

The idea of "blind spots" inspired me to write a series which I entitled, "Eye-Ear Communication." We are dealing with the "No See Zones" of truck drivers and "No Hear Zones" for people with hearing loss.

Truck drivers encounter numerous blind spots or no see zones that can cause accidents or create other transportation problems. When vehicles or objects go out of sight, they cannot be seen by the truck driver. No hear zone for persons with hearing loss occurs when he/she cannot see your face.

Driver visibility to the operator is when the driver can see all

> *Just because you can't see my hearing loss it doesn't mean that it doesn't exist. Please understand that I do have a hearing loss and need your help to communicate. I must see what you say.*

vehicles around his semi-truck. There are places where vehicles are hidden from the view of the driver. Most accidents happen in these areas.

A sign on the back of a truck reads, "If you can't see my mirrors, I cannot see you." It basically interprets that the burden of safety is on the vehicle behind the truck and not on the truck driver. Drivers must become familiar with these blind spots and drive accordingly.

From the sign on the back of the truck, I coined the statement: "If I can't see your face, I can't understand you." Anyone not facing the person with hearing loss is in the no hear zone.

Speaking out of earshot means you are in my no hear zone. I may hear sounds, but I cannot distinguish the words or meaning. If you don't get my attention first, then I don't understand you. Speaking first without facing me is a "lose-lose" communication situation.

It is crucial that you understand and practice where my no hear zones are every day. When you get out on the road, you meet those big trucks mile after mile. You must practice safety with every one of them. Failure to face any person with hearing loss in the no hear zone means bad communication.

It is the hearing person's responsibility to know what to do in the presence of friends with hearing loss. You cannot blame people with hearing loss for not understanding you if you are not facing them. It is an essential need for clear communication. We do appreciate it every time.

Blinding Lights Can Hinder Hearing

Blinding lights can hinder hearing because you can't see the speaker. Friends with hearing loss need to see the speaker's face at all times for good communication. In the illustration of truck drivers having blind spots, there are other things that can blind the driver also. Oncoming lights can be blinding as well as light from behind, shining in the mirrors. So it is with people who depend on lip reading.

Glaring light can prevent people with hearing loss to communicate properly. Those with good hearing rarely think of hearing loss as blind spots. We assume that everyone can hear in all kinds of conditions.

There are four areas that can hinder a listening experience. Lighting is a major problem for people with hearing loss.

1. Lighting from behind the speaker can be a hindrance. There are many settings where the speaker has his back toward the light. Sunlight or daylight coming through a stained glass window can be blinding to a lip reader and make it impossible to see the

speaker's face in the light's shadow. In outdoor meetings, I have encouraged the speaker to face the sun, so the audience does not have to squint to see the speaker. With individual speakers, see if you can move away from the light or switch positions. To hearing people, this does not seem to be a problem because they do not depend on lip reading. They can even close their eyes and listen.

2. Tiny lights and chandeliers can cause blind spots for those who are trying to hear by seeing. There is nothing more aggravating than having to stare at those tiny lights on the wall behind the speaker. In some churches, lights above the choir are blinding. It is exhausting trying to read the speaker's lips and stare at pinpoint lights.

    Christmas lights or decorative lights can be hard to the eyes. Chandeliers can create problems for lip readers. I am not opposed to fancy lights, but not in places where lip reading becomes difficult. It is best not to have chandeliers past the first row of pews. In a church I visited I went up to the balcony. To my surprise, I was above all the chandeliers in the church; that was a lip reading nightmare for me.

> A rule of thumb for every speaker is to ask the audience, "Can you see me, clearly?"

3. Standing in front of a power point or overhead projector screen can create a shadow on the speaker's face. When a missionary shows slides, the church lights go off, and background music begins. It is impossible to read lips. When you have a good projector, it is not necessary to turn down the house lights.

4. Poor lights on the speaker can be a blind spot for lip readers. The speaker has no idea if the audience can see his/her face clearly. Some churches have a spotlight shining down on the podium for

the speaker to see his notes. It may create a shadowy effect on the speaker.

A simple solution would be to have spotlights on both sides, so the speaker is clearly visible. Sometimes a flood light on the floor can create a pleasing atmosphere for those who read lips. Good lighting is vital for better communication for friends with hearing loss. It is a reasonable service to be able to accommodate those who need to see the speaker's face.

A rule of thumb for every speaker is to ask the audience, "Can you see me, clearly?" The best method is for the speaker to scan the audience to make sure he/she can see everyone's face. Always be conscious of the fact that some people in the audience cannot hear as well, and therefore it is necessary for them to be able to have a clear view of the speaker. Remember in order to hear and enjoy the speaker they must see.

Obstructions Can Hinder Hearing

Blind spots to hard of hearing people happen when disconnected from the line of vision with the speaker. People with hearing loss depend on hearing and seeing the lips of the speaker. When they can't see the speaker's face, the line of communication is broken. It is important to understand where these blind spots are and change your communication strategy.

There are blind spots for truck drivers while driving on the highway. When a vehicle enters into this blind spot, the truck driver cannot see the vehicle. This disconnects the vehicle from the line of vision. The greater responsibility for safety falls upon the vehicle in the blind spot. It is important to know where those blind spots are and move cautiously. In a similar way, those with hearing loss can experience blind spots of communication. Here are a few of those blind spots:

1. When the speaker turns sideways to point to an object or turns his/her back to write the line of vision disconnects for the one

with hearing loss. It is done naturally, without even realizing, and one may ask, "What's the big deal?"

The University of Georgia passed a law stating that a teacher cannot talk while writing on the board. The students could not comprehend important details with the teacher's back turned.

Teachers must write on the board without talking and then turn around to the students and lecture.

A group of hard of hearing students persued this issue until it became a reality. Every classroom should practice this. It is the speaker's or teacher's responsibility to understand this concept of communication for those with hearing loss.

2. One cannot begin talking to a person with hearing loss without first getting his/her attention. I have to warn people constantly, "If you didn't get my attention first, I didn't hear you." It is necessary that you make sure that you are in the line of my vision before you speak to me. It means that you cannot start speaking from behind or from another room. You may have to move closer to the hearing loss person. "This takes too much time to do," you may be saying. I understand, but it takes more time to repeat something again. It is an act of love and consideration for people with hearing ability.

3. Looking down at the computer or a book while talking and giving instructions does not work. We do this out of habit and never think that we are disconnecting our communication line of vision for people with hearing loss. A simple solution for this situation is to look up directly when speaking, keep the line of vision clear.

4. Whispering in the ear of a person with hearing loss creates a double-blind spot. It is impossible to read lips and to hear voiceless words. If the message is a secret, then it is best to go out of the room where you can speak out loud.

5. Speaking only a single syllable word is an unusual blind spot even if you are speaking face to face with a person who has hearing loss. Some words do not register. The ear and the eye still have

problems distinguishing certain words. Here is an example where a single syllable word can be confused. You may say, "Get me that bat." The word "bat" looks and sounds the same as mat, pot, and pan. Are you asking for that baseball bat? That floor mat? That flower pot? Or that frying pan?

6. Another blind spot is when a speaker says to turn to a page or a leader says turn to verse. While I am frantically turning to that page or verse, the speaker continues talking. I have been disconnected from the speaker while searching for that page number or verse. Information has been lost, and I have no clue what I'm supposed to know.

It is best to put statements or verses on power point so those with hearing loss can concentrate on the speaker's message. Pastors who like to have the congregation look up a dozen verses while speaking lose me. In most cases, the verses will be read from the pulpit, so why bother to look it up?

These are just a few blind spots that the hearing loss person encounters regularly. You cannot expect everyone to know all the blind spots. Be sensitive and understanding. The people with hearing loss will appreciate every effort you make to connect with them.

Communication Gaps Hinder Hearing

Blind spots of hearing or communication gaps of persons with hearing loss occur in the damaged cell of the cochlea. Damaged hair cells receive incoming sounds but send garbled messages to the brain. Hair cells are damaged forever, and we misunderstand so much even when wearing a hearing aid.

We can compare the blind spots a truck driver faces with the communication gap of missing words in a person with hearing loss. I understand better that hearing miscommunication is multifaceted, not just one thing that causes us to misunderstand words in communication.

A person with mild hearing loss can miss up to 45% of a normal conversation. A missionary to Russia explained that he still misses about 50% of the language spoken, after ten years of study. As a person with a severe to profound hearing loss, I miss 75% of a normal conversation all the time.

In some countries, the triangle sign is displayed to warn drivers of problems or blind spots on the road ahead. Signs in the U.S. warn of hidden driveways, trucks entering the highway, a stop sign or a traffic light ahead.

Blind spots may occur inside the cab of a truck, causing hazards. The A-pillar or windshield pillar and interior rear-view mirror can block a driver's view of the road.

Visual information travels along the optic nerve in the eye before it journeys to the brain for processing. A certain spot on the optic nerve does not have any receptor cells (the area where the optic nerve leaves the eye) and, as a result, can't receive information. The result is the blind spot.

Those of us with hearing loss can experience a disconnection in our line of communication in six ways:

1. Words are hard to follow when they are not given in a natural conversational mode. It is too difficult to read the lips of singers to understand the words because they tend to drag out vowels. The instrumental accompaniment also makes it hard to concentrate on the message sung. Vocal music is a lost world for me without written words.

2. Background music while someone speaks creates havoc with the communication process, as in videos, movies, and restaurants.

3. Someone praying from the platform or the audience without a microphone becomes inaudible. Taking questions or requests from the audience is a disaster for me. When someone prays with his/her head bowed it makes it impossible to read their lips.

4. Speaking in the dark while showing slides or a power point or even speaking from off stage is hard to follow.

5. Foreign speakers pronounce words with an accent. Some of them speak fast or with different lip movements.

6. Speakers who pace back and forth away from the microphone are hard to follow. Some speakers walk amidst the audience to make a point. If I am sitting on the front row and he/she walks behind me, I cannot hear what is being said.

> **The greater the hearing loss, the more a person relies on vision rather than hearing aids for total communication. 60% of speech sounds are impossible to see or understand in lip reading.**

You can never assume when you speak, that you are heard and understood well by everyone!

To comprehend spoken words, friends with hearing loss depend on simultaneous communication methods in conversation. This method includes:

- Hearing the voice with or without a hearing aid
- Facial expressions and lip reading

- Visual augmentation
- Possibly written texts or finger spelling

Take the keyboard or your computer. For efficient typing, the keyboard must be memorized. Many people have not learned the keyboard but use the hunt and peck method of typing. It can slow you down, but what if three keys lost their letters or identification symbols? Three blank keys could slow you down even more.

You depend heavily on letters to be on the keys because you are using only sight to type. This comparison is fitting for friends with hearing loss.

Communicating with a hearing loss requires total observation and focus. It is exhausting, yet a privilege to participate in any group discussion. We must never give up.

Adjusting to new equipment can be a blind spot for those with hearing loss. It takes time, patience and persistence to get adjusted to a new hearing aid or hearing situation. It may seem strange at first.

Every day presents a new challenge for hearing. Every place you go has challenges that make it difficult to understand what is being said.

It's like a truck driver getting introduced to a brand new rig with enormous size, length, width and overwhelming weight. There is a period of adjustment and understanding what the big rig will and can do as well as getting acquainted with all the buttons, gauges, lights, and sounds. It not only takes time, but practice.

When you get a new hearing aid, all the new sounds are overwhelming. Slow down and get acquainted with the buttons, remote, size, and sounds. Your brain has to assimilate this new environment of hearing.

Now is not the time to quit and stop wearing your hearing aids. It is not the time to stop going to social groups, entertainment centers, church services or school. The hearing aid will not benefit you hidden in the dresser drawer, purse or pocket. I have been guilty of this myself, leaving my hearing unit at home instead of wearing it. I have been in an important business meeting or social situation and realized I was missing too much. So, I put new batteries in my hearing unit and gave it another chance.

With my head up high, I began to tackle hearing situations with gusto. I was determined to wear my aids for three months, seeking to work out a solution for each challenge I faced. Time is too precious for me to avoid networking meetings, church services, training classes, socials and a host of other events.

You can learn to make adjustments that will improve communication wherever you go. Remember when you first started driving a car? So many adjustments to make: starting the car, shifting, stepping on the gas pedal, stopping, staying in your lane and avoiding the curbs. Soon the adjustments will become natural movements.

When I was in college, I acquired a job driving a school bus. I had never driven a bus before and had not been assigned a route. One day another driver came to me and asked if I would drive his bus route at 2:30 p.m. I panicked when I discovered it was a seventy-two passenger bus. He handed me the keys and left me standing with my mouth open. It was noon, and I had to learn how to drive the big bus.

The buses were parked at the Minnesota State Fairgrounds across from the college campus. Entering into the bus, I felt I was inside a train car. The steering wheel seemed to be three feet in diameter.

I was to be at the school by 2:30 p.m. I drove to the school, after two hours of double clutching, shifting, moving forward and turning corners while running over curbs, to pick up the children. I learned that day; persistence is more important than quitting. When you quit you surrender to the problem, but when you persist you conquer the problem. Every day presents new challenges. You have a lot of living to do, make adjustments and keep on going. I know you can do it!

Avoid All Blind Spots of Hearing

Friends with hearing loss must be on high alert. They have to observe what is happening around them at all times, watch where sounds are coming from and identify movement that produces sounds.

High alert for those with hearing loss means they need to be awake to function at an energetic level to anticipate any problem that may occur. Take our eighteen wheeler truck drivers, checking every mirror, direction and gauge inside the cab. It is required to scan all gauges every three to six seconds, look out all mirrors every four to eight seconds and then they must look ahead at the road every twelve to fifteen seconds.

These guidelines apply to all pilots, bus drivers, train engineers, race car drivers and ship helmsmen. Traveling at high speed commands our attention constantly. Accidents can happen quickly without warning.

Walking from a parking lot to a large church we had to cross a busy street. A police officer was on the opposite side directing pedestrians. As an elderly lady stepped out onto the lane, a car hit her. The dear lady did not hear the officer holler, "Stop!" because she was hard of hearing. Sadly, the accident was ruled her fault. I wept over that situation; it should never have happened.

More accidents are happening because people are busy on their cell phones, texting or listening to their iPods. As persons with hearing loss, we must be on guard at all times. We want our independence, but we also want to breeze through communication roadblocks when we meet them. Always be aware where you can go and hear and know where you cannot hear. You may have to create your hearing space or the hearing accessible situation. Know what you need to function in a social situation and make adjustments.

Be aware that you will deal with situations that will be difficult for hearing. If you enter a room full of people, move into a position that will help you hear. Whenever I attend a conference or a teaching session, I arrive early to choose the best seat for myself. The best place for me is near the speaker and also where I can see most of the people in the room. When people interact with the speaker, I want to see who is speaking.

> **You may have to create your hearing space or the hearing accessible situation.**

Prior to the meeting, I meet the speaker or teacher and explain my hearing loss needs. I ask if he/she would assist me with these simple things: face the audience, repeat questions from the floor and to write on the board and then talk.

This strategy works well in medical facilities where your name or number is called: doctor's waiting rooms, airports, fast food restaurants.

For your information, remember the infamous oil spill by the Exxon Valdes? The helmsman, Robert Kagan, suffered from hearing loss and did not hear the orders to turn the ship. He never told anyone for fear of losing his job. Perhaps, this may have happened on the Titanic ship, where thousands died. The inability to admit the hearing loss and request assistance is common to many dear friends with hearing loss.

Potholes, Roadblocks, and Detours

Life with hearing loss can be a bumpy road for all of us. It is not always smooth communication. Every bump becomes a major issue and great struggle. Communication is a day to day challenge.

For hearing impaired, there seem to be many setbacks and disappointments. The way you face them can make all the difference in the world.

In writing this book, *Lord, You Know I Can't Hear*, I have experienced many bumps, potholes, and roadblocks. It appeared that this project would never get done. It is the same communicating with others.

Waiting upon the Lord can be just as frustrating when I want to move ahead with speed. I feel impatient and make hasty decisions, creating greater setbacks. Too many well-meaning friends sent me on a road leading nowhere. Everyone wants to give advice to improve hearing, but in the end it may lead to nowhere.

With every roadblock and shutdown, I realize God has a reason for everything. It is His testing time for me to discover something I need to put in the book.

My hearing impaired friend, take heart, this is not the time to give up and quit. We must keep on moving forward to make progress in life.

A detour ahead leads to a smoother road of communication. An alternative route can make life better for you. How you accept the challenge determines the outcome ahead. Always be prepared to try a new idea of communication to help you personally. Attitude is important to reach the goal of better hearing. Forget all the things others have done to you. The future is as bright as the promises of God.

> "But as it is written, Eye hath not seen, nor ear heard, neither have entered into the heart of man, the things (plans, miracles, blessings, methods, ideas or new ways) which God hath prepared for them that love him." I Corinthians 2:9 (Note words in parenthesis are my interpretation.)

5

Two International Signs for Disability

There are two international signs for disability. In 1990, George H. W. Bush signed into law the American Disability Act (ADA) and adopted both of the international symbols as the standard signs for America. These symbols are required to be blue in color and are an indication of information for the public to see and heed.

Two Signs

The wheelchair accessible logo is seen everywhere we go, in parking lots and on the front of buildings. Wheelchair accessibility or access means reasonable accommodation. This law deals with mobility. Without this law in place, people in wheelchairs would be barred or excluded from most public places.

The hearing accessible logo is the second international symbol adopted into law along with the wheelchair logo. To my knowledge, I have never seen this sign in any public building. The public does not know that reasonable accommodation for people with hearing loss covers some amplification. This law deals with communication. Without this law in place, people with hearing loss would be barred or excluded from people. Communication for people with hearing loss is essential for living, working and social life. People with hearing loss are disconnected from the world of people, without hearing accommodation or assistance.

Two Needs

The wheelchair law deals with architecture or access to buildings, bathrooms, hospitals and entertainment centers and the design of streets and curbs. It means putting ramps and elevators in older buildings.

The hearing accessible law deals with technology that enhances communication. This law may include methods and strategies of communication in order to become fully hearing accessible. Some disabled, hearing people have personal devices such as hearing aids, but these devices are not adequate in public places. Loudspeakers hanging from the ceiling is not sufficient for the needs of those with hearing loss. The technology needed is a personal device that connects the speaker to the ear of those who struggle with hearing loss.

Two Evidences

The wheelchair law is a physical thing. Getting into any building is a major issue and needs to be addressed. It is obvious when you see someone in a wheelchair that he/she has a handicap.

The people with hearing loss have an invisible handicap not recognized in public. The problem is with being able to hear the speakers. Since the public does not see any evidence of hearing loss, they may assume that everyone hears perfectly.

Two Voices

The people in wheelchairs are vocal about their need for access to buildings. They do not have to say much because their dilemma is obvious. Lawsuits have sprung up everywhere over accessibility or access to the public facility. The wheel that squeaks the loudest gets the most attention.

The disabled hearing community has remained non-vocal when it comes to their need for hearing accessibility. No one wants to be singled out as a disabled person. They do not want to use or try out an assistive listening device in public for fear of embarrassment. Silence is the major issue when it comes to helping hearing disabled people in public or church.

Two Populations

Wheelchair Population

In 2002, the U. S. Census estimated that there were 2.7 million wheelchair users living outside medical institutions. Wheelchair users are among the most visible members of the disability community. They experience the highest levels of activity limitation and functional limitation that have the lowest levels of employment.

Mobility is the key issue for them. One of the major obstacles involves transportation. Today there are special elevators, wheelchair lifts and handicap vehicles like accessible vans. There are positive trends in public transportation as well. In 2007, some 98% of transit buses were equipped with ramps.

Hearing Loss Population

The hearing loss population is exploding at a phenomenal rate. There are more than 50 million people with hearing loss. The group has doubled in ten years and expects to double again in the next ten years. Hearing loss is a major international health issue that has become uncontrollable.

Two Guidelines

Since 1990, the wheelchair regulations and guidelines have been applied to 80,000 buildings of state and local government and more than seven million public places within the first ten years. Today, all new buildings must adhere to the city and state wheelchair access code. The regulations and guidelines have been placed for hearing accessibility. If the hearing disabled people won't speak up and make their needs known, how can we help them?

The ADA rights of hearing accessibility for the hearing disabled people do not take effect until we ask for it. We need to unite our voices to make our request known.

Two Decisions

The American Disabilities Act exempts churches from complying with the law for hearing disability, yet 20% of every congregation in America has a pocket of people with hearing loss that impacts the church. We can make one of two decisions:

- The first decision is to deny that this handicap exists and do nothing about it. We can force hearing disabled people out of the church by negation, hoping that will solve the problem. It works like a magnet. When two magnets come together, they are drawn together with force. When the poles are reversed, the magnet repels. Some churches may treat disabled hearing people in this manner.

- The second decision is for the hearing disabled people to speak up and ask for hearing accessible help. When we do not make our needs known to hear the Word of God, nothing is done. Why spend money on a project when there is no request for it? It is vital for us hearing disabled to speak up. People with hearing loss can start a "Hear Now Revolution" in the church or house of worship. Discuss your needs and decide what you want and present it to the board.

A great paradigm for mission work is to start in the local church and begin reaching out into the community. When you meet the needs of the hearing disabled then they will hear the Word of God clearly.

 This sign has been created by, Let My People Hear, Inc. as a plea to make churches hearing accessible. The church is the best place to start. Every church in America has a pocket of people who suffer hearing loss. Form a hearing loss support group, discuss what your needs are and bring them before the church.

A Rabbi friend who wanted to make the synagogue hearing accessible created this sign or symbol to share with Jewish friends with hearing loss. They are hearing accessible for the public to come and hear the Word of God.

Life can be difficult for those who have hearing loss if we cannot enjoy daily communication. Active communication is $9/10^{th}$ of life and is our greatest concern. Hearing is the lifeblood of our social life and is weakened when we cannot practice it.

6

The Birth of the Magic Hearing Button

For years, I have been trying to develop a better way for people to communicate with me. I find it frustrating to repeat over and over that I have hearing loss. If I could find a simple way to improve my communication, then I could teach others.

I discovered a simple technique that could be put into practice immediately: The Magic "Hearing" Button of communication for friends with hearing loss. The Magic Button is more than a neat little item to wear, but a powerful story to be told. The Magic Button is your badge of authority and a legal document that must be respected. It is your personal hearing accessibility sign that can radically change your world.

Hearing loss is one of the most prevalent chronic health conditions with 50 million Americans hearing disabled. They are the largest special needs population with serious quality-of-life and accessibility issues according to the World Health Organization (WHO).

Once you appropriate the method, your burden will be lightened. Hopefully, most people will try to help you hear and understand.

I have been profoundly hard of hearing (legally deaf) since birth and have depended on lip reading and closed captioning. In 2006, I began searching methods to help those with hearing loss to hear better without spending a fortune. In the last seven years, I developed an alternative method of hearing and communication.

Thomas Edison was urged to give up on inventing the light bulb because people already had gas lights. Edison declared, "There are no rules here-we're trying to accomplish something." After 10,000 experiments, he found the solution to create light from electricity.

I felt tempted to give up my idea of creating an alternative method of hearing and communication. My breakthrough came on Monday, September 9, 2013, a giant leap in communication for people with hearing loss around the world and all languages: The Magic Hearing Button.

Hearing loss is called the runaway handicap because very little is being done to help people cope with their hearing loss. "Hearing loss is on the front edge of an epidemic," reported Dr. Roland Eavey in the Journal of the American Medical Association. The National Institute on Deafness agrees that the findings are significant and says the next step is moving beyond analysis.

Unaddressed hearing loss often leads to isolation, anxiety and depression. Untreated hearing loss is more noticeable than wearing hearing aids.

"If you have poor hearing your brain almost has to work harder to decode and process sounds. If your brain is having to reallocate resources hearing, it probably comes at the expense of cognition or thinking ability," says Dr. Frank Lin of John Hopkins University.

When using headphones, personal music players can subject listeners to noise levels similar to those of jet engines. Noise levels exceeding 110dB (decibels) are known to cause hearing problems such as temporary hearing loss and tinnitus (ringing in the ears). With the first long time exposure, the hair cells in the ear are damaged. To continue this path of listening to excessive volumes can lead to greater irreparable hearing loss.

Most adolescents appear to know the risks of exposure to loud music but are rather reluctant to accept advice from others.

Every member of your family, coworkers and friends are affected by your hearing loss. You cannot hide your hearing loss by acting as if it did not exist.

Magic is the art of producing an effect or controlling events. Magic is the general term for any supposed art of producing marvelous effects. A trick is the art, method or process of doing something successfully or getting specific results quickly. This chapter is a gift from God to help stir up your heart and faith.

To develop a skill is stronger than strength. The skill to do something comes by doing. "Doing easily what others find difficult is talent; doing what is impossible with talent is genius," says Henri Frederic Amiel.

Helen Keller said, "I am just as deaf as I am blind. The problems of deafness are deeper and more complex, if not more important than those of blindness. Deafness is a much worse misfortune. For it means the loss of the most vital stimulus—the sound of the voice that brings language, sets thoughts astir, and keeps us in the intellectual company of man." She continued, "Blindness separates us from things, but *deafness separates us from people.*"

> *"Children who hear acquire language without any particular effort; the words that fall from others' lips they catch on the wing, as it were, delightedly, while the little deaf child must trap them by a slow and often painful process. But whatever the process, the result is wonderful. Gradually from naming an object we advance step by step until we traversed the vast distance between our first stammered syllable and the sweep of thought in a line of Shakespeare."*

And he said unto them, "He that hath ears to hear, let him hear." Mark 4:9

The art of praise does wonders for our sense of hearing and well-being. Dr. E. H. Mayo stated, "One friend, one person who is truly understanding, who takes the trouble to listen to us as we consider a problem, can change our whole outlook on the world."

There are several steps to take before the magic of the button works for you. The magic button has no power in itself. With it you can improve communication skills and prevent a lot of misunderstandings. Note the progression to make the magic work for you.

Receive the button and pin it above your heart. Study and develop your script or story that you want to share. Practice and practice again with your family and friends until the story becomes second nature, and you are comfortable with it. Start out gradually and soon you will be able to go public and perform your story. Persistence makes the impossible possible. It is said, "It is not the voice that commands the story: it is the ear."

The Magic "Hearing" Button method is for people who need help with their hearing. The button has no power in itself to restore hearing. The strategy or formula behind the button can work wonders for all who apply it to their daily lives.

When it comes to hearing better for the hard of hearing, it is not more gadgets, surgery, medicine or technology, but rather a unique technique that is needed. The technique is the secret behind the Magic Hearing Button that helps your ability to communicate increase dramatically.

The most expensive hearing aid in the world may fail to bring back your hearing, and more hearing equipment may disappoint you. Take the time to read this chapter several times, so you can grasp the concept and put it into practice.

Develop a bold attitude, become an advocate and be assertive for your hearing loss. Draw attention to the button to take the focus away from yourself, if you feel shy or intimidated about your hearing loss. Just tap on the Magic Hearing Button and the words will explain your need to hear and understand.

Tell your story of the Magic Hearing Button and most people will listen and assist you. The button will not help you if you don't wear it. A big step for our hard of hearing friends is deciding to wear the button at all times, in public as well as at home. You are not the only one in the world with a hearing loss. Be brave! You can do it!

Let's get started! Take the button out and pin it over your heart while reading this book. **If you did not receive a button with this book, please refer to the order form located in the back of the book.**

The Magic Hearing Button

Let me share the story about the magic hearing button and explain three things on the button.

First of all, the background symbol is the international symbol of hearing disability. It is equivalent to the wheelchair sign we see everywhere. The button is your announcement that you have a hearing loss. The symbol is your request for reasonable accommodation as written by law in the American Disabilities Act of 1990.

The symbol is a legal announcement, to include stricter guidelines that were revised in 2010. The law states that public venues must provide reasonable accommodation for those disabled in any form. Rejecting the request for accessibility is now considered a federal felony and can be subject to a lawsuit. Please note that a person with hearing loss cannot be fired. You can request assistance to make your job easier to perform.

Second, the button has two statements on it. The first part says, "FACE ME," a request for the speaker to slow down and speak within your hearing range. It challenges the speaker to accommodate your communication needs. "If I don't see your face, I cannot hear you or understand fully your words."

The second part of the statement is an explanation, "I LIP READ." You focus intently on any speaker who approaches you. When your hearing goes down, you watch the faces of people closely. The statement, "I LIP READ," places the speaker in the right position for better communication, within three to five feet and in good lighting, facing you.

The third thing about the button is your personal story. What type of hearing loss do you have? How long have you been hard of hearing? What caused the loss? Do you have tinnitus or ringing in the ears?

What percentage of hearing loss do you have? Which ear is best or worse for hearing? Do you wear a hearing aid? How do you want me to speak to you?

Advocating for People with Hearing Loss

When one becomes an advocate, he must become a spokesman for the disability of another person. For the hard of hearing, someone needs to be a supporter to inform others to communicate properly so that the hard of hearing can understand the flow of conversation.

Here are eight things to consider about advocating for the hard of hearing:

1. Advocate for yourself. Speak up when communication becomes difficult in any social situation. Tell the group that you are hearing impaired and need to see who is speaking. Tell them how much you appreciate being included in the discussion.

2. Advocate for others. When there are others with hearing loss in the group, you start advocating for them, supporting your friend, as well as yourself. A faithful friend and advocate are like medicine to the heart. It seems easier to be an advocate in a group situation than to toot your own horn for yourself.

3. Train others to advocate for you. Train a friend or mate to advocate on your behalf. Encourage someone like a co-worker to remind others that you have a hearing problem. Let them know how they can include you in the discussion.

4. Be a model advocate. When I am asked to introduce myself to a group of people, I treat the entire group as if they were hard of hearing. I explain that all people with hearing loss depend on lip reading and need to see the face of the one speaking. Remember we are hard of hearing 24/7. Just because someone is speaking does not mean that everyone can hear perfectly.

5. Advocate by letter. Write a letter about your hearing problem and what you want others to do for you. Send your letter by email, snail mail or pass it around to co-workers and friends. Post a copy on the bulletin board or the mirror in your home.

6. Advocate with leaders. Before any event, it is best to speak to the leader, speakers and moderators who can accommodate your personally. Most people are caring and will help in a diplomatic way.

7. Advocate with placards. In a large Bible class, the leaders forgot that there were hard of hearing people present. The speakers would wander from the microphone making it difficult to hear. Comments from the audience were impossible for me to hear.

   I decided to help the cause by creating several 8 ½" by 11" placards or signs to be held up at the appropriate times. My signs were: "Louder Please," "Use the Microphone," "Repeat the Comment," "Face the Audience," "Who is Talking?" and "Thank-you." It brought the attention of everyone to those with hearing loss in the group.

8. Let the Magic Button advocate for you. To discover the Magic Hearing Button was the thrill of my life. I experimented with all the above methods and this little two ¼" button is the most powerful advocate I ever used. The average hard of hearing person will not speak up for himself or others in the group. To remain silent means that you will not understand what is going on. Develop strategy that works for you and will include you in

most conversations. Friends will feel proud of you when you speak up. I know I will be proud of you.

12 Ways to Use the Magic Hearing Button to Enhance Hearing

When you wear a Magic Hearing Button, it becomes your spokesman and authority for attention and opens communication wherever you go. The magic may be a mystery, but watch it work for you.

Here are 12 areas where the button can help:

1. Entering a busy office where the secretaries are multi-tasking. Get the secretary's attention, point to the button and explain that you are hard of hearing.

2. In the waiting room of the doctor, ask the secretary to remind the nurse to come and get you rather than calling you from across the room.

3. In the examining room, inform each person who enters about your hearing needs.

4. In noisy restaurants when the waitress begins to quote the specials of the day, ask her to slow down and come closer or show you the menu.

5. In a registration line when the questions are fired at you rapidly. Explain that you are hearing impaired and ask them to accommodate you kindly.

6. When being interviewed in an office, the director is sitting at a desk with a window behind. Explain that the light is blinding and could hinder your lip reading. Reposition yourself or ask for the blinds to be closed.

7. In any group conversation, be up front that you need to know the topic and who is talking. Have someone advocate for you by keeping you informed or taking notes.

8. When stopped by the police show the button and explain your hearing problem. Ask the officer not to shine his flashlight in your eyes. The button is a legal symbol and should be acknowledged and respected. Explain that you do not use sign language, but lip read.

9. Waiting in the airport can be the worst nightmare. It is difficult to hear announcements given over the loudspeaker. You could ask the announcer to wave at you or come and get you. When I discovered the disability line for those who needed special assistance, my Magic Hearing Button became my "passport" to get in that line.

10. Seating at conferences. When there are no reserved seats, I arrive early enough to get permission to sit near the speaker. If you arrive late, this would not be possible. Plan ahead.

11. In the dental chair, let the dentist know you need to see his face when he speaks. He may have to pull his mask down. It is important for anyone wearing a mask attempting to communicate to you.

12. In the hospital as a patient, you can put the Magic Hearing Button to work for you. Anyone who enters your room needs to know you depend on lip reading to understand them.

Find the answers to the problems of communication for people with hearing loss. Become proactive about your need to hear and understand what people are saying. Train yourself and others to understand the communication situations they face. The Magic

Hearing Button offers potential for proactive improvement by your advance preparation.

Put in place an auditory training idea to make the most of what you hear. Adjust your hearing aids. A person with mild hearing loss may miss 45% of a conversation and much more in a telephone situation.

Train your eyes to augment what you hear. With speech reading and lip reading, you can increase your comprehension by 30%. You may not need to buy more technical equipment or expensive hearing aids. The magic hearing button empowers you to be more assertive in making your hearing needs to be known.

You may feel desperate about finding a better way to communicate. If you feel you want to seclude yourself from society, find a better way to help others communicate with you. Try to discover what the missing element is that would help you to understand what people are saying.

> **Are you brave enough to forget what people think about your hearing loss and experiment with an alternative method of better hearing and communication?**

You may be wearing hearing aids, but still find communication and comprehension difficult. You might even be considering an expensive upgrade or a cochlear implant. To help in your social situations, you depend on technology.

You want to improve your communication skills, so you bought this book which promotes The Magic Hearing Button: a new paradigm for people with hearing loss. Welcome to our non-technical method that supplements hearing aid technology. Read this entire book carefully.

Are you brave enough to forget what people think about your hearing loss and experiment with an alternative method of better hearing and communication? Make a serious decision about better communication at home, in social settings, the classroom, the church, and everywhere you meet people.

I Can't Tell Anyone I'm Hard of Hearing

Phyllis came to the Lip Reading Academy to get help with her hearing loss. She wanted to overcome some of the daily challenges of communication. Her greatest challenge was in a weekly Bible study and prayer time in a ladies group at a local church. She was having difficulty hearing the comments and prayers coming from the ladies and became discouraged. She nearly dropped out of the Bible study.

At the Lip Reading Academy, we stressed the importance of telling others about your hearing loss. Phyllis responded, "I can't tell anyone I'm hard of hearing. What would they think of me?" My only reply was, "Then you will continue to suffer in silence and drop out."

As the training session continued, we re-emphasized the need to speak up and make your need to hear known to others. The burden is on each of us to make our hearing loss public. It doesn't do any good to keep it a secret. Later Phyllis was very excited to tell about what had happened in the Bible study class the week before. She told the following story:

"I stood up and told the ladies I had a confession to make." Reaching up and pulling out a hearing aid and holding it up, she said, "I am hearing disabled and have difficulty understanding everyone." It was eerily silent for a moment. A shock wave of sudden understanding went out over the ladies as they gasped in dismay. Several ladies responded, one at a time, "I too wear hearing aids and have trouble hearing in the group." An older lady said she was surprised that a person younger than her admitted a hearing loss and said, "Why didn't I think of that before? Now I am going to get my ears tested and get a hearing aid." Another lady came and thanked Phyllis for declaring her hearing loss publicly. The lady also thought she might need a hearing aid, as well.

Phyllis discovered that she had no reason to hide her hearing loss, nor be ashamed admitting it. She was then able to assist the entire group by making changes so everyone could see, hear and understand everything spoken. It made a world of difference for this ladies group.

Most fears we have about exposing our hearing loss are self-inflicted. Your friends are caring and will understand your hearing need and want to help.

The "Leper's Cry!" of the Hearing Impaired

People with hearing loss must constantly be warning or telling others that they are hearing impaired. If you want to hear and communicate, you will need to inform the people you meet of your disability.

> **People who cannot hear well are often cursed or tagged with names like "retarded", "slow" or "stupid"... These are "stones" that drive the hearing impaired out of the church and public life into isolation and separation from their loved ones.**

In biblical times, there is a story of the laws for people who had leprosy. In the book of Leviticus, there is a story that relates to me. It's the account of a person who suffered from leprosy. Here are the guidelines outlined in Leviticus 13: 45 & 46.

> *"As for the leper who has the infection, his clothes shall be torn, and the hair of his head shall be uncovered, and he shall cover his mustache and cry "Unclean! Unclean!" And he shall dwell alone; his dwelling shall be outside the camp."*

The "leper's cry" of the Bible sounds somewhat like the cry of the hearing impaired. "I'm hard of hearing! I can't hear, I have a hearing loss," is our cry whenever we meet people. We must constantly inform others of our need to communicate.

Lepers were excluded from the place of worship by law and required to go into isolation from the public. They became outcasts to their friends and loved ones. One requirement of the law was to announce loudly, "Leper! Leper!" so that people would clear out of the way. That is the leper's cry.

Tradition says that if a leper got too close to other people, they would curse him and throw rocks at him.

A parallel to the hearing loss community; people with hearing loss are a stigma that society does not want to handle. Should hearing disabled people be separated from the hearing public and not be allowed to interact? It seems easier just to avoid them. People feel frustrated when they do not know how to communicate with those who have a hearing deficiency.

People who cannot hear well are often cursed or tagged with names like "retarded", "slow" or "stupid." And statements like, "He only hears what he wants to hear" or "He has selective hearing or is dumb." These are "stones" that drive the hearing impaired out of the church and public life into isolation and separation from their loved ones.

They may feel shunned in the workplace, schools, playgrounds, parties and socials and often in their families. Churches fear that accommodating hard of hearing will draw too many of those so-called "strange" or "odd" people. Handicaps are not always well accepted because it seems like too much work to be a blessing to those people.

Friends with hearing loss need to declare their disability in public places. Everywhere I go, I tell people, "I have a hearing loss. Please face me; I lip read." My family is constantly telling others that I am hard of hearing, and it is crucial to get my attention first. I feel like the leper crying out, "I have low hearing! I'm hard of hearing," all day long. If I do not speak up about my hearing loss, communication is more difficult.

I would rather stay home than attend a church service, Sunday school class, Bible study or prayer meeting where I can barely understand what is going on. I feel driven into isolation because I cannot function in a hearing world.

In the year 2007, the Lord impressed me to start a ministry called, "LET MY PEOPLE HEAR Inc.", to encourage churches to include hard of hearing in all programs and activities of the church. We are on a crusade to create hearing accessible environments wherever people gather.

In the 14th chapter of Leviticus, the writer declares the "Law of the Leper," giving extensive instructions on reclaiming lepers back into the church and society. It is a great day when a leper is healed and restored to normal life again.

Today there is very little written in the American Disabilities Act (ADA) on how to include the hard of hearing in the church and public life. Let's open the church doors and welcome the hearing impaired into our fellowship. Let's offer them reasonable accommodation for hearing the communication.

Beethoven's Confession

Beethoven lost his hearing at age 27 and stayed in the no hear zone for the remaining years of his life. He was too embarrassed to tell anyone of his hearing loss. He became suicidal, but his passion for writing music kept him going. I have copied this from Wikipedia in part. This is an English Translation.

"For my brothers Carl and (Johann) Beethoven.

Oh, you men who think or say that I am malevolent, stubborn, or misanthropic, how greatly do you wrong me. You do now know the secret cause which makes me seem that way to you. From childhood on, my heart and soul have been full of the tender feeling of goodwill, and I was even inclined to accomplish great things. But, think that for six years now I have been hopelessly afflicted, made worse by senseless physicians, from year to year deceived with hopes of improvement, finally compelled to face the prospect of a lasting malady (whose cure will take years or perhaps be impossible).

Though born with a fiery, active temperament, even susceptible to the diversions of society, I was soon compelled to isolate myself, to live life alone. If at times I tried to forget all this, oh how harshly was I flung back by the doubly sad experience of my bad hearing. Yet it was impossible for me to say to people. "Speak louder, shout, for I am deaf." Ah, how could I possibly admit an infirmity in the one sense which ought to be more perfect in me than others, a sense which I once possessed in the highest perfection, a perfection such as few in my profession enjoy or ever have enjoyed. —Oh, I cannot do it; therefore forgive me when you see me draw back when I would have gladly mingled with you.

My misfortune is doubly painful to me because I am bound to be misunderstood; for me there can be no relaxation with my fellow men, no refined conversations, no mutual exchange of ideas. I must live almost alone, like one who has been banished; I can mix with society only as much as true necessity demands. If I approach near to people, a hot terror seizes upon me, and I fear being exposed to the danger that my conditions might be noticed.

Thus, it has been during the last six months which I have spent in the country. By ordering me to spare my hearing as much as possible by an intelligent doctor... But what a humiliation for me when someone standing next to me heard a shepherd singing and again I heard nothing.

Such incidents drove me almost to despair; a little more of that and I would have ended my life-it was only my art that held me back. Ah, it seemed to me impossible to leave the world until I had brought forth all that I felt was within me. So I endured this wretched existence —

truly wretched for so susceptible a body, which can be thrown by a sudden change from the best condition to the worst.

Patience, they say, is what I must now choose for my guide, and I have done so – I hope my determination will remain firm to endure until it pleases the inexorable Parcae to break the thread. Perhaps I shall get better, perhaps not; I am ready. –Forced to become a philosopher already in my twenty-eighth year, -oh it is not easy, and for the artist much more difficult than for anyone else.-

Divine One, thou seest my inmost soul thou knowest that therein dwells the love of mankind and the desire to do good.

Oh fellow men, when at some point you read this, consider then that you have done me an injustice; someone who has had misfortune man console himself to find a similar case to his, who despite all the limitations of Nature nevertheless did everything within his powers to become accepted among worthy artists and men.

Farewell and do not wholly forget me when I am dead; I deserve this from you, for during my lifetime I was thinking of you often and of ways to make you happy – be so.

Ludwig van Beethoven
Heiglnstadt,
October 6th, 1802

A great man who believed he was imperfect wrote this very sad letter. His work kept him alive until he finished his greatest works.

A Son's Confession

Betty, now in her seventies, had completely lost her hearing and since then received two cochlear implants. It was hard for her to adjust to life with a hearing loss. To get through difficult communication situations she depended on her son Chad. Chad at age 51 began losing his hearing due to Meniere's disease but refrained from telling his mother. Betty had observed that he was struggling with hearing loss. Returning from the ENT doctor, Chad was very depressed that he too was going deaf. Betty confronted her son and asked, "Why didn't you tell me you were losing your hearing?" With tears in his eyes he responded, "Oh Mom, I knew my hearing was going, but I don't want to be deaf like you."

There is help all around if you would accept it. Acceptance is the most difficult thing to do when you fear the worst. Most people who struggle with an oncoming handicap may wait for years before they can accept their lot in life. Brave people will own up to their disability and then deal with it and may even turn it into a ministry by helping others with the same handicap.

One time we came upon a bird fluttering on the ground from an injury. I reached out my hand to help the bird to safety and protection. The bird jerked away in an attempt to escape my help. I was the only one who could help, but the bird refused my assistance and would soon be at the mercy of another animal.

> **Brave people will own up to their disability and then deal with it and may even turn it into a ministry by helping others with the same handicap.**

On another occasion, we encountered a baby bird that had fallen out of the nest. Naturally, I wanted to help the little bird get back into the nest. The mother bird began screeching and attacking us to leave her baby alone. Similarly, some people deal with hearing loss in this way, they refuse help and resist assistance to deal with their disability.

Why do people who need help refuse it? It is my mission and passion for helping people who suffer hearing loss. In the church, I am conscious of those who visit that are hard of hearing. You can tell if they are wearing a hearing aid or they cup their ear with the hand. The natural thing for me is to offer one of our, "FM assistive listening devices," to help them hear during the service. Instinctively, the response is, "No, I can hear just fine." Over the years, I have discovered deeper reasons for not accepting the FM unit in public. Here are some of the thoughts and rationales: "What will people think of me if I plug that earbud receiver in my ear?"

"I don't want to appear as an old feeble person. "

"I am too proud to let people know that I need help to hear."

"I've never tried an FM device; it may not help me."

"People may think that I am a little slow and my I.Q. has slipped a few numbers."

I offered the husband of a couple seated in the church an FM hearing unit. He looked at it and started to take it; his wife interrupted and said, "Don't embarrass me. If you stick that thing in your ear, I'm leaving." How sad when family members keep others from hearing the Word of God.

7

The Secret of Lip Reading

Hard of hearing people need to see a visual manifestation of the spoken word. Which includes lip reading, facial expression, written text and other types of visuals. Such help has a tremendous impact on the hard of hearing community.

Observing lip movements, facial mimicking and body language may help the hearing impaired person understand what is said. Listening with both ears and eyes does not come naturally, but demands effort and endurance.

Lip reading on the person speaking is what captioning is to TV. It takes time and practice. Lip reading can best be developed in supportive groups and environments such as family and friends.

The learning process never ends. No two people read the same. Faces and dialects vary, but the more you learn, the greater your confidence, and the better your ability to communicate with the hearing world.

Learning lip reading takes time, patience and understanding, but the rewards are worth it. Always invite people to look directly at you and talk naturally.

Here are some tips to facilitate lip reading:

- Get in a position so you can see the speaker's face in good lighting.
- Relax and be comfortable in the conversation.
- Detect the tone of speech and articulation of words by the movements of the mouth.
- Ask the speaker to rephrase a word or sentence when you do not understand.
- Note the speaker's facial expressions. You can gain a lot about the subject and mood.
- You can gain clues from the speaker's gestures, such as nods, pointing and glances in other directions.
- Make sure you understand the subject of the conversation. Words are easier to understand when you know the context.

- When a person begins to lose hearing, it is only natural that he watches people's faces. Hard of hearing must find an alternative way to understand what people are saying.
- Visual information from the face, tongue and lip movements provide clues about the spoken message and enhance the intelligibility of speech.
- Note articulations that accompany the production of speech sound. Using my eyes to hear improved my communication skills.

Teach yourself the technique of reading lips. When we speak, we never give thought to how words form in the mouth. In reading lips, we must develop the habit of knowing precisely how each word forms. We must consciously and mentally see the position of every sound.

With lip reading, we are taking the English language to a higher level by learning the physical mechanics of the spoken word. Once we get the proper formation, it is a matter of repetition until it becomes a habit.

It is not necessary to tell anyone that you are lip reading. Just ask people to face you so you can hear. Tactile language learning is a training style in which you learn by teaching yourself by identifying every movement or position the spoken word makes.

Every sound spoken requires some fifteen to twenty different muscle movement. Each word has its distinct formation and placement. These positions are critical in identifying words. I am talking about the placement of teeth, tongue, lips, throat, cheeks, eyes, chin, chest, brow, head, nose, and jaw. There is the muscle sense or the sensation by which movement perceives.

You can teach yourself the lip reading technique by thinking how each word forms. Talk to yourself and identify what muscles move to create a word. Mimic or imitate words people are saying. Teach your brain to recognize those word formations. It will come to you as you practice. No two people will say a word the same way. You will see similarities from person to person.

Helen Keller, who was both deaf and blind, was asked, which would you rather be, deaf or blind? She answered, "I am just as deaf as I am blind. The problems of deafness (or hearing loss) are much deeper." (I added the hearing loss line.)

I ask you, friend, which is even more challenging, to be deaf or hard of hearing? Are they the same? Or are they different challenges?

For hard of hearing, life remains challenging because we live among hearing peers. Hearing people cannot fully understand our hearing loss. Hearing loss is often sadly pegged as "selective hearing, or you are just playing games!" Can a person turn off his hearing at random and deliberately miss things?

We tend to feel paranoid from all the put-downs, and isolated when not included in the hearing activity. We can become socially maladjusted. If we, who are hard of hearing, want to be accepted by the hearing world, we must inform others of our communication needs.

We must explain what we need from the hearing world in six areas:

1. Tell them you are hard of hearing, and you lip read.
2. Wear a button that says, "Face me, I read lips." Even if you do not read lips, people will move closer and speak to your face.
3. You must always be training and teachers others on what you can hear and what you miss.
4. Show others your audiology report to explain why you miss certain tones or sounds.
5. Produce a letter explaining some simple things that would help you to communicate.
6. Practice the way you want others to speak to you. Show them what works best for you.

I Speak Lip Reading

I speak lip reading. It is a language all its own. How can that be? If American Sign Language is the second language for the deaf, then lip reading is the second language for the hard of hearing. Both are a part of the natural language for disabled people.

As "seeing ears" are eyes to the blind, so "hearing eyes" are ears for the hard of hearing. The eyes become the third ear for the hard of hearing and ears become the third eye for the blind. Lip reading takes the English language to a higher level through visualization of words. You already know the language; now you will learn it from the visual point of view.

The speaking voice moves dozens of muscles per second for each sound spoken. The average person does not think of all the movements that go into producing a word or a sentence. We will analyze the various movements for sounds and show each student how to teach himself the art of lip reading. There are some simple techniques to make this happen.

941 colleges across America are teaching American Sign Language to 91,000 students. Gallaudet College in Washington, D.C. has reported that only 500,000 deaf Americans speak sign language. There are more than 50 million Americans who suffer mild to moderate hearing loss and need help communicating with lip reading. No college in America offers lip reading as an alternative to sign language. Most hard of hearing people do not want to learn signs because there is no one available to speak with them.

Lip reading can be useful anywhere, anytime with anyone in any language. It is important to understand that lip reading needs to take place within close range in order to be effective.

Before babies can speak clearly, they can read people's lips and understand some basic signs. When introduced to a young child or baby, I resort to a soft voice and use visual lip movements.

What captioning is to TV and movies, so lip reading is to the hard of hearing, whether live or in film.

There are four components to lip reading that will improve your communication skills.

First there is what you see with your eyes, the facial and lip movements, and expressions. There is also body language and animation of the speaker.

The second part is what you hear. 98% of people with deafness are hearing impaired, in other words, they have some residual hearing. These people depend on some amplification such as hearing aid, pocket amplifier, wire loop system, infrared or FM listening system. And sadly, there are also those who are not aware of any technical devices to improve their communication ability.

The third component of communication deals with techniques and strategies. If you do not have a hearing aid, you can improve your hearing by as much as 30%. The Lip Reading Academy presents a number of simple methods that can enhance anyone's hearing ability. These ideas can be applied as you understand them.

The fourth component seems the most precarious. When all the above fail then you can take chances and guess what you may have missed. This method can cause problems and miscommunications. Making a mistake in what you thought you heard may lead to arguments, fights, and hurt feelings. There is a solution to this method. Tell others that you have a hearing loss and did not understand the message or word spoken. Ask them to repeat what was said and thank them for their help.

Lip reading, also known as [lipreading] or speechreading, is a technique of understanding speech by visually interpreting the movement of the *lips* face and tongue when normal sound is not available. Relying also on information provided by the context, knowledge of the *language,* and any residual hearing.

Lip reading allows you to "listen" to a speaker by watching the speaker's face to figure out their speech patterns, movements, gestures, and expressions.

The greater the hearing loss, the more a person tends to rely on vision in order to understand speech. Benjamin Franklin said, "When you speak to another person look them in the eye, when the other person speaks, look him in the mouth."

Lip reading is facial linguistics in which the grammar of movements of the body and face helps to understand the spoken language. It does not work well when words are sung as with musicals.

When a person is unable to communicate in a group situation, he tends to withdraw from the social situation and go into seclusion away from public.

Sign language (also signed language or simply signing) is a language that uses manual communication and body language to convey meaning, as opposed to acoustically conveyed sound patterns. It can involve simultaneously combining hand shapes, orientation and movement of the hands, arms or body, and facial expressions to fluidly express a speaker's thoughts.

Learning American Sign is not for the deaf who want to speak with other deaf. They already know the language. Learning lip reading is not mainly for hearing people, but for those who have hearing loss so that they can converse and communication with the hearing world. It does not make sense for the deaf to take classes in ASL (American Sign Language).

The hearing loss people of America need to learn a second language to improve communication, a language that enhances his mother tongue and one that assimilates into his natural speech pattern without effort. Lip reading is now the second language of the people with hearing loss and those who are deaf. They are not in the same language bracket or category. Deaf interpreters are few and far between. Lip reading is the second language of the hearing impaired and is everywhere.

Lip reading can be self-taught by practice and by watching other people. You are a marvelous creation of God with thousands of facial nerves and muscles. These muscles are controlled by thought. In fact you speak, and the muscles move automatically. You don't have to think about it. Each word you speak already knows how to form and shape the mouth. Each word has its unique formation and position that can be identified by sight.

Teach your brain those positions so you can identify them. Begin by shaping words with your mouth slowly to understand all the movements it takes to say a word. Think of all the movements of the face, mouth, lips, tongue, throat, forehead and neck. You don't need to know any scientific or anatomy names for this. Watching yourself in a mirror is a good method.

For fun, speak with pronounced emphasis or exaggeration in slow motion. Identify what is happening at the moment. Now speed up the words as fast as you can, noting the formation is the same.

Read out loud on purpose to get the feel of the language. Lip reading is possible in any language. People of all ages can do it. Babies read lips before they can speak. Animals are known to read lips of certain commands.

Whenever someone is speaking to you, start imitating their lip movements. All lip shapes of words are the same everywhere. Ask family or friends to talk to you silently. If you can't hear the voice, your observation is intensified. You may not understand every word, but you get an idea of the topic.

Lip reading cannot stand alone as a complete language in itself without voicing. 60% of any spoken language, including tonal languages is not visible on the face.

8

Hearing Loss, a Mission Field

About 800 million people around the world are affected by hearing loss. Estimated, this number will rise to 1.1 billion by 2015, which is about 16% of the world's population. (http://www.phonak.com)

Hearing loss is one of the most prevalent chronic health conditions with 50 million Americans hearing disabled. They are the largest special needs population with serious quality-of-life and accessibility issues according to the World Health Organization (WHO).

Hearing loss is called the runaway handicap because very little is being done to help people cope with their hearing loss. "Hearing loss is on the front edge of an epidemic," reported Dr. Roland Eavey in the Journal of the American Medical Association. The National Institute on Deafness agrees that the findings are significant and says the next step is moving beyond epidemiological analysis.

Unaddressed hearing loss often leads to isolation, anxiety, sadness and depression. Untreated hearing loss is more noticeable than wearing hearing aids. "If you have poor hearing your brain almost has to work harder to decode and process sounds. If your brain is having to reallocate resources to hearing, it probably comes at the expense of cognition or thinking ability," says Dr. Frank Lin of John Hopkins University.

What will it Take?

What will it take for the church/Christians to realize that people with hearing loss compose one of these largest untapped mission fields in America?

The number of Americans who suffer mild to moderate hearing loss is rapidly rising to 100 million due to self-inflicted hearing loss. Only 1.5% of these people are fully deaf and speak sign language.

90% of the hearing loss population may not attend church for one reason. The church is not hearing accessible for them to hear the Word of God clearly.

Some pastors will exclaim, "We have assistive listening devices in our church, but no one uses them." Great! How much advertising do you do to promote the listening system? Does the public know about it? Do visitors know where to go to get a listening system? Is the listening system active and functioning?

Are your Bible study and prayer groups hearing accessible? These are critical issues to consider if you want to reach the masses with the gospel of Jesus Christ. Becoming a hearing accessible church is the most cost effective way to create a revival spirit in the community.

You do not have to learn a new language, just make a few adjustments in attitude and willingness to minister to those with hearing loss. A number of them are already members of your church who have dropped out because of hearing loss.

There are millions of friends with hearing loss at your doorsteps waiting to be invited in to hear the gospel. They will listen, believe and be saved if they can hear with the assistive listening devices. It is a massive untapped mission field waiting for harvest. Let us begin the work while it is still day.

A Pastor's Response to the Call

Pastor Bob Humphreys made visits to church members at Erlanger Medical Center one Sunday afternoon. Finishing his last visit, he headed down the hallway. A nurse ran after him, asking, "Which church are you pastoring?"

"Edgewood Baptist Church on 27th Avenue," he replied with a smile.

"My husband dropped out of the church because he can't hear clearly or understand the message," Nurse Cathy relayed, with concern in her voice as she briefly shared.

"You tell your husband, I want to see him in our church next Sunday," Pastor Humphreys challenged the nurse.

My wife, Nurse Cathy, convinced me to attend church with her at Edgewood Baptist. After church, the pastor came to us to learn more about my hearing loss. At that time, I did not have any advice to offer to help someone hear clearly. Pastor Humphreys closed the discussion with a request, "David, I want to see you back here next Sunday."

I drove to Edgewood Baptist Church the following Sunday, and the pastor called me up to the platform. He handed me an FM hearing receiver with an earpiece to hear the morning message. "This unit is for you to use every time you attend this church," Pastor Humphreys explained.

What a delightful experience to hear the Word of God clearly from the pulpit! This amazing technology was a wireless Personal PA, FM Listening System designed for churches or audiences of any size without any distracting background noise. The unit picked up the message and relayed it to anyone using the system. These hearing devices pick up sound up to 1000 feet away from the speaker.

I returned to church for the evening service with great anticipation to hear the Word of God clearly again. The pastor opened the service, asking the congregation if anyone had a blessing or testimony to share. I jumped up to share in a jubilant voice the joy of hearing the Word of God through the FM unit. "Pastor, you sound so good to me, I can hear you loud and clear."

When the service ended, two men approached me and wanted to see the FM unit. Both men asked me, "Why can't we have these hearing units?" As a second time visitor, I couldn't answer the question. Both men marched up to the platform and asked the pastor about the FM units.

The following Sunday (my third visit), Pastor Humphrey called those two men to the platform before the congregation. "These hearing units are for you to use in church," he explained. "At the end of each service, give the units to David and he will take care of them." I was now given a volunteer job on my third visit to the church.

That evening, the pastor opened the service, asking again, "Does anyone have a blessing or a testimony to share?" The two men from the back pew spoke out about how happy they felt to hear the Word of God clearly. This scene repeated itself over a two-month period until fifteen people with hearing loss each received a hearing unit, in a congregation of eighty-five members. There may have been more people with hearing loss who did not ask for a hearing unit, but could have benefited greatly. All they had to do was ask.

> Every church in America has a pocket of people with hearing loss who need some assistive hearing device (ALD). For every deaf person in America, there are 97 persons with mild to moderate hearing loss. 85% of these people do not attend a church service or Bible study because they have difficulty hearing the speaker clearly.
>
> Over 50 million Americans suffer mild to moderate hearing loss, the largest untapped mission field in America.

An Opportunity Not an Obstacle

My wife, Cathy and I, were invited to attend a Bible class at a church on a Sunday morning. It was a small room with fifteen people seated in rows. The leader met and greeted us warmly. I handed him a business card and noticed he was wearing two hearing aids, so I asked about his hearing loss. He had lost his hearing working in a factory.

As the class session began, the teacher asked me to say a few words about my ministry. I shared: "We are in the ministry of helping people who lost their hearing and want to regain it so they can hear the Word of God clearly in the Bible study classroom." I went on to share that hearing accessibility in the classroom is simply this: "Make sure that every person can see, hear and understand everything spoken in the room." I asked how many people had a hearing loss or were wearing hearing aids. Reluctantly, six hands went up. I asked if they had problems hearing and understanding what went on in the classroom and many responded affirmatively.

When speaking to any group, my goal is to make sure everyone can see my face. It is the number one rule in good communication with people with hearing loss. I noticed the couple in the second row, where the man with two hearing aids was not looking at the speaker. He was in an "isolation daze" of boredom because he was not getting the message. Instinctively, I began to wave my hand to get his attention. He seemed oblivious to what was going on. The class leader interrupted and said, "Do not pay any attention to him; he cannot hear."

I was stunned, and I started to weep visibly. What? Half the members of this class have a hearing loss, and no one cares if they hear the Word of God? There sat a man, who could not hear the Bible lesson; this broke my heart with great sadness.

That gentleman had just as much right to hear what was going on in this class as the hearing people. You can make some simple changes in how you communicate to include all the people with hearing loss in the classroom. People with hearing loss need to stop acting like hearing people and make their request known by making simple adjustments for the benefit of everyone present. This is not an isolated case in one church. Every Bible class in every church will have members who struggle to hear the Word of God, but will not speak up and make their hearing needs to be known.

On Monday morning, I went to the pastor and poured out my heart over this oversight in one classroom. It indicated to me that there were people within the church that needed assistive hearing units.

"Would you let me come and offer my service to minister to those with hearing loss for free?" I asked. The pastor indicated that the church could not take on any other mission projects, presently, but maybe later. I left with a broken heart for the people with hearing loss in that church. An opportunity had just turned into an obstacle for the hearing impaired.

One out of every five members has a definite hearing loss severe enough for them to drop out of the church. The offering plate will be short because of their absence. For every person with hearing loss in the church, there are estimated 97 people with hearing loss outside the church who may come if they knew that the church was hearing accessible. Beloved, the largest untapped mission field in the country is the hearing disabled group. Jesus said in John 4:35....

> *Say not ye, There are yet four months, and then cometh harvest? behold, I say unto you, Lift up your eyes, and look on the fields; for they are white already to harvest.*

Ignorance Causes Rejection

John, a middle-aged blue collar worker, belonged to a Community Church and tithed faithfully. John had a severe hearing loss and wore hearing aids. He stopped attending the main service in the sanctuary for two reasons, the music was too loud and hurt his ears and because he found it difficult to understand the pastor. John felt discouraged and decided to sit in the lobby during the main service and read his Bible and pray. He continued to attend the small group Bible studies and found these enjoyable.

One morning several elders of the church came to him asked him to go into the sanctuary for the worship service. John explained that he had a hearing loss and could not understand the message. If the church had an FM hearing system for hearing impaired, he would return to the services. The elders promised to talk to the pastor and the board regarding this need.

I visited the pastor to explain the situation. The pastor reminded me that the church could not afford to purchase an FM hearing system for one hearing impaired person. The board would not approve it.

The next month the elders returned to talk to John in the lobby. They expressed their disappointment in John's behavior, insisting that he was a disgrace to the church body and disrespectful to God by not attending the main worship service.

"You cannot sit in the lobby during the worship service," the elders said. "If you will not attend the service, you have to leave the church."

This is not the kind of compassion Jesus had in mind when He commanded us to,

> "...Love one another; as I have loved you, that ye also love one another." John 13:34

Unfortunately, this sad situation reappears differently in other churches. I spoke in a church about opening the doors to the hearing impaired. 80% of the hearing impaired do not attend church because the church is not hearing accessible. The leader's wife approached me after the service and remarked, "We are not going to invite a bunch of weirdos to our church." My response was that 20% of the congregation was already hearing impaired. "Are they all weirdos?" I asked.

People with hearing loss are not a lesser class of the human race. They can do everything but hear and constitute the largest untapped mission field in America. What an awesome opportunity we have before us! Hearing accessibility means to love and care for those who cope with hearing loss. It is time to embrace and educate ourselves and our churches to reach out to those who suffer hearing loss. Ignorance and an unwillingness to be a part of the solution is not bliss or acceptable.

My Heartfelt Prayer

One beautiful Sunday morning, The Lord impressed upon me to bypass Sunday school class and slip into the peaceful sanctuary to pray that hour for our pastor and his message. I asked God to show His presence in this lovely church and that decisions would be made, lives transformed and hearts healed.

Musicians quietly discussed music for the morning service as I sat in the last pew under the balcony, admiring the stained glass windows with sunlight streaming. I opened my Bible to Matthew 13 to read the story of the sower. I noted that the word 'ears' mentioned five times and the word 'hear' nineteen times. I read verse 23:

> *But he that received seed into the good ground is he that heareth the word, and understands it; which also bears fruit, and brings forth, some an hundredfold, some sixty, some thirty.*

My heart felt stricken. If our hard of hearing friends cannot hear and understand clearly the Word of God, there can be little or no fruit in our lives. I looked out over the silently waiting pews and prayed. "O my gracious, loving Father, It would be so wonderful if our hard of hearing friends could hear and understand the precious Word of God given in this place, so they could bear fruit for the Lord."

My tears flowed as I cried out to the Lord,

> "O God of infinite, eternal love, what about the hundreds and thousands of dear souls who live in this area and cannot hear the Word of God clearly enough to understand and bear much fruit? Which church would accept them into its family? Who will show compassion and build a ramp of hearing accessibility? Where can they find a hearing accessible Sunday school class? Who will take the time to help them understand the Word of God?

O my Heavenly Father, let me be an instrument in your hand to help them. Please, MOST HIGH LORD, use me to reach out to many hard of hearing for your glory. O Merciful Heavenly Father, my heart feels broken for their vacuum of silence. My burden stays heavy to help them. Grant my request quickly, O Lord Almighty, send your favor, blessing and miracle of love upon our pastors and churches. Amen."

9

Creating a Hearing Accessible Church

n 1990, the American Disabilities Act was signed into law. We assumed that it was for people confined to wheelchairs. There was pressure to make their places of business wheelchair accessible. The law required curbside ramps, special parking places, large entryways and bathrooms with rails for the handicapped.

Should the Hearing Accessibility be included in the church? As a mission outreach? Churches began to comply with the law and followed the requirements. They have built outside and inside ramps, elevators, special doors and parking spaces. All this effort for people in wheelchairs, but where are these special people today? How big is the wheelchair population in America? Can we estimate one in a thousand, five hundred or a hundred? We have been in scores of churches and have seen one or two wheelchairs at the most. What happened? Is there no longer a need for this type of ministry? Did we build those ramps because it was the law or out of love for someone in need?

The ADA exempted churches and non-profit ministries from the law. What you may not know is that the ADA includes other disabilities and handicaps. The largest disability group in the country is hard of hearing people. 50 million people in America suffer from some degree of hearing loss. This group will double in size to 100+ million in the next decade. The alarming thing is that the medical profession, the public nor the church is prepared to accommodate these people.

We are at a critical moment in the church to do something to reach the hearing impaired. In every congregation in America, one out of every five members has a significant hearing loss and needs some hearing accessibility assistance. What is even more shocking is that more than 80% of those with hearing loss will not attend church, a Bible study or a prayer meeting because they cannot function in a hearing world. For example, in the state of Tennessee there are 350,000 hard of hearing people waiting to attend a church that is hearing accessible. They are in every neighborhood in the state.

Every church has an untapped mission field outside its doors. With a few simple adjustments, we could begin to grow our congregations.

These hearing disabled people have nowhere to go unless someone invites them. We as Christians need the wisdom to do what is right and honorable for these dear people. A little compassion can go a long way in bringing glory to the name of our LORD.

The church needs to consider becoming a hearing accessible place that is hearing friendly for people with hearing loss. There needs to be some visible evidence that this church cares about those with a special need to hear. Create a **hearing center** with a simple FM listening system for the hearing impaired to use during the service. The whole purpose of the **hearing center** in the church is to help people who have lost hearing and desire to hear the Word of God clearly. The major expense would be the purchase of an FM listening system with enough units to meet the needs of the congregation and visitors who attend.

Some churches have Assistive Listening Devices (ALD), yet few people use them. Why don't members use them when they are available? We have found several large churches that have the listening system, yet the hard of hearing people rarely ask for them. One in five church members has hearing loss. The need for hearing is still great. How do we get people to use them? Here are six things that may help you understand the problem.

1. **Understand that buying a listening system,** whether FM, telecoil loop or infra-red system is not a "cure-all" for the hard of hearing. It is the beginning of becoming a hearing accessible church, not the end. We are hard of hearing in every department of the church, not just in the main sanctuary.
2. **Promote that you have a system in the sanctuary.** Every time I board an airplane, I sit through a demonstration on floatation devices, exit doors, and oxygen masks. Perhaps one thing we can do in the church is to announce publicly that the system is

available and where units are located. There should be signs on the wall, reminders in the bulletins and the newsletter, and attachments to all forms of advertisements. If you want to attract hard of hearing people to the church, spread the word that you have this wonderful system for anyone to use. Tell former members who stopped attending church due to hearing loss. You have family members, relative, neighbors, or co-workers who want to enjoy the services but don't know where to attend.

3. **Overcome the stigma of hearing loss** to the hard of hearing members in the church. Wearing an earpiece or a headset does not mean that you are old, deaf or retarded. No one will think less of your or make fun of you. Did you come to hear the Word of God and be blessed?

4. **Remember that it takes up to seven years** before a hard of hearing person decides to get a hearing aid or try out the system. It is very hard for people to admit that they are losing their hearing and need help. Be patient and do not nag. Nagging may drive people away.

5. **Keep the system running** and ready for people. Have the system turned on during the service and keep fresh batteries in the receivers. The units need repair when they break down. Someone should be in charge of this service.

6. **Store the hearing devices** in a place where the public can get to them safely. We have found them in a janitor's closet, in the electrical room, overstuffed cupboards, junk drawers and an old wire basket where all the units were messy and tangled together. The hard of hearing people deserve better than this. My dream is to have a cupboard out in the foyer or at the welcome center set up like a post office. Each unit is numbered, cleaned and ready to go. They can be sanitized to be clean for use. We want a first class system. Let my people hear with dignity.

My challenge to you is to become known as the church that cares for the hearing impaired. They are the largest untapped mission in the country. Make simple adjustments to meet the needs of those with hearing loss.

> *...behold, I say unto you, Lift up your eyes, and look on the fields; (neighborhoods); for they are white already to harvest. John 4:35*

Order the Magic Hearing Button

Hear smarter with the Magic Hearing Button.

Behind this unique button is a technique to improve your hearing skills by as much as 30%

This is the solution that I have been seeking for over nine years.
It was so simple that I am amazed how powerful it is.
The button is self-explanatory but must be told with your story

Order your Buttons today. Sold in pairs in case you lose one. Full instructions are included with every set. Pin it on and let it begin working for you.

Cost $5.00+ $2.00 for shipping. Total $7.00
Send a money order to **Let My People Hear, Inc**. with your name & address to P.O. Box 3021 Chattanooga, TN 37404

Order online: letmypeoplehear.com then click Button

Contact letmypeoplehear@yahoo.com or 423-624-1669

MAGIC BUTTON ORDER FORM

Customer Shipping Address

Contact Name

Street Address

Street Address
Line 2

City

State

Zip Code

Phone Number

Email Address

Order Information

The Magic Button ($5.00 + $2.00 shipping)

Quantity   **X $7.00**

Total

Make money order payable to:
Let My People Hear

Send To:
Let My People Hear, Inc.
P.O. Box 3021
Chattanooga, TN 37404